MICKEY ROGERS
JOANNE TAYLORE-KNOWLES
STEVE TAYLORE-KNOWLES

SPEAK YOUR MIND

STUDENT'S BOOK
+ access to Student's App and Digital Workbook

2A

macmillan education

	Outcomes	Vocabulary	Grammar	Speaking
Unit 1 Extraordinary pp. 7–15	• Discuss role models • Talk about a memorable event • Write and talk about an anecdote	• Role models • Reactions • Family situations	• Past progressive • Past progressive vs. simple past Grammar Reference pp. 142–143	• Discuss events in a timeline • Describe personal events • Share anecdotes
	Language and Life—Communication: Present a Citizen Award			
Unit 2 Party! pp. 17–25	• Talk about an idea for a holiday • Talk about money and spending habits • Write about a celebration	• Unique holidays • Money and shopping • Food and drink packaging	• Quantifiers • *enough / not enough* Grammar Reference pp. 143–144	• Talk about new holidays • Discuss opinions about celebrations • Share ideas about special foods
	Language and Life—Creativity: Create a Graduation Ceremony			
Unit 3 What's Trending? pp. 27–35	• Talk about street entertainers in your area • Discuss activities of the past • Write and talk about viewing habits	• Street entertainers • The music industry • TV viewing	• Indefinite pronouns • *used to* Grammar Reference pp. 145–146	• Discuss street entertainers • Compare generations • Talk about TV viewing habits
	Language and Life—Decision-making: Design an Event to Save a Theater			
Unit 4 Your ID pp. 37–45	• Talk about personality types • Describe people with superlatives • Talk about who you are like	• Personality types • Different personalities • Characteristics	• *(not) as … as* • Superlative adjectives Grammar Reference pp. 146–147	• Describe a person's personality • Talk about your personality • Compare family members
	Language and Life—Interpersonal Communication: Understand and Interact with Different Personalities			
Unit 5 Prepping pp. 47–55	• Make predictions and express intentions • Make requests and ask permission • Talk about a social event	• Checking in • Making suggestions • Wedding customs	• Modals of intention, offer, and prediction • Modals of request and permission Grammar Reference pp. 148–149	• Role-play a conversation • Describe plans for a class party • Talk about a social event
	Language and Life—Global Competence: Understand and Appreciate Social Customs			
Unit 6 Changes pp. 57–65	• Talk about risk and change • Discuss life experiences • Discuss positive and negative effects of changes	• Status quo • Life experiences • Changing cities	• Present perfect with *for* and *since* • Present perfect with *ever* and *never* Grammar Reference pp. 149–150	• Discuss changes in your life • Talk about life experiences • Debate changes in your town
	Language and Life—Collaboration: List Recommendations for Visitors Discovering Your Town			

Confident Communicator	Pronunciation	Listening/Reading	Thinking Skills	Writing
Start Talking • Language for speculation *Repair It* • Replacement words *Start Talking* • Sequencing words	• Vowel + consonant + *e*	Read a biography • Skill—Skim a text Listen to people recall memorable events • Skill—Listen for specific information Listen to a story about look-alikes • Skill—Predict the story	• Evaluate • Analyze • Understand	Write an anecdote
Unit Review p. 16 **Study Skills** p. 127—Using Personal Experience				
Keep Talking • Give reasons *Start Talking* • Give opinions *Keep Talking* • Ask follow-up questions	• /tʃ/ and /ʃ/	Read about unofficial celebrations • Skill—Predict the topic Listen to a conversation about the business of holidays • Skill—Identify opinions Listen to a Chinese dumpling recipe • Skill—Listen for specific information	• Analyze • Evaluate	Write about a celebration
Unit Review p. 26 **Follow A Pro** p. 128—A Hotel Manager ▶ An Event Planner				
Start Talking • Make notes *Keep Talking* • Ask for opinions *Keep Talking* • Qualifying phrases	• Reduced form of *used to*	Read a magazine article about street entertainers • Skill—Identify main ideas Listen to an interview with a music producer • Skill—Listen for numbers Listen to a recording about TV viewing habits • Skill—Identify opinions	• Understand • Evaluate	Write about your viewing habits
Unit Review p. 36 **Study Skills** p. 129—Designing a Questionnaire				
Keep Talking • Show disagreement *Keep Talking* • Talk about life events *Keep Talking* • Make comparisons	• Stress on the adjective in *as … as* / *not as … as*	Read an article about personality types • Skill—Summarize Listen to a lecture about personalities of a team • Skill—Identify tone Listen to a recording about family personalities • Skill—Listen for detail	• Apply • Predict	Write about a movie character
Unit Review p. 46 **Follow A Pro** p. 130—A School Psychologist ▶ A Teacher				
Keep Talking • Useful phrases *Keep Talking* • Make requests *Start Talking* • Practice giving a talk	• Word stress with modal auxiliaries	Read a dialogue about a hotel reservation • Skill—Scan Listen to a conversation about a class party • Skill—Listen for gist Listen to a conversation about wedding etiquette • Skill—Listen for main ideas	• Predict • Remember • Analyze	Write about weddings
Unit Review p. 56 **Study Skills** p. 131—Organizing to Help Memorization				
Keep Talking • Useful phrases *Keep Talking* • Reacting to information *Keep Talking* • Point of view	• Present perfect contractions	Read an article about status quo bias • Skill—Identify examples Listen to a recording about bucket lists • Skill—Listen for main ideas Listen to a radio show about changing cities • Skill—Listen for specific information	• Analyze • Create • Understand	Write about your city
Unit Review p. 66 **Follow A Pro** p. 132—An Architect ▶ An Urban Planner				

Grammar Quiz: What Do You Already Know?

A Complete the conversation with words from the box.

are is 'm not 's 's what's

Esme: Hi, my name's Esme. **1** ___________ your name?
Monique: My name **2** ___________ Monique.
Esme: Nice to meet you, Monique. Where **3** ___________ you from?
Monique: I **4** ___________ from France. I work here. I'm an interpreter.
Esme: Really? That **5** ___________ interesting.
Monique: It **6** ___________. I love my job! What about you? Are you American?
Esme: No, I'm **7** ___________. I'm British.

B Complete the paragraph with the simple present form of the verbs in parentheses.

My sister, Emily, really **1** ___________ (love) her phone. She **2** ___________ (check) her phone when she **3** ___________ (wake) up. I think she **4** ___________ (send) about a hundred text messages a day! She **5** ___________ (use) about five different social media sites, too. I **6** ___________ (have) a smartphone, too, but I can live without it. I **7** ___________ (not need) to post pictures of my food every time I have a nice meal! What about you? How much time **8** ___________ you ___________ (spend) on your phone?

C Choose the correct option.

Leo: What **1 do you have** / **are you having** for lunch today, Jill?
Jill: Today **2 I'm having** / **I have** noodle salad with shrimp and chili sauce.
Leo: It looks delicious! **3 Did you buy** / **Do you bought** it from the café?
Jill: No, **4 I made it** / **I'm making it** at home. It's cheap, and it's healthy, too.
Leo: I think I **5 should** / **could** start to bring food from home. The cafeteria always **6 serves** / **serving** the same things. I **7 want to** / **want** eat a more balanced diet.

D Find one error in each line of the conversation. Write the corrected sentence.

Rob: Is you almost ready, Julie? **1** ______________________________
Julie: Yes! I'm so excited about going to the Amsterdam! **2** ______________________________
Rob: Where do you want to do when we're there? **3** ______________________________
Julie: I want to go sightseeing around a city. **4** ______________________________
Rob: Yeah, I like to do that, too. Can we go by bicycle? **5** ______________________________
Julie: I'd like to, but I can ride a bike! **6** ______________________________

E Complete the email with words from the box.

a a her 's the the X (no article) your

Hi Malu,

Thanks for your email! I'm really excited about **1** ___________ school trip to France next summer. **2** ___________ hometown looks beautiful. It's great that there is **3** ___________ waterfall just three kilometers away. Is there **4** ___________ forest, too? I love **5** ___________ trees! Can we climb **6** ___________ mountain you told me about? I know the weather is sometimes rainy in France, so I've borrowed my friend **7** ___________ waterproof jacket and I've also borrowed **8** ___________ walking boots.

See you soon!

Reba

Go to the Grammar Review on pages 140–141

UNIT 1

Extraordinary

WHAT DO YOU ALREADY KNOW?

1 **What extraordinary people do you know? Write their names, countries, and careers in the box.**

2 **IN PAIRS** **Share and compare your words. If possible, add more words to the box.**

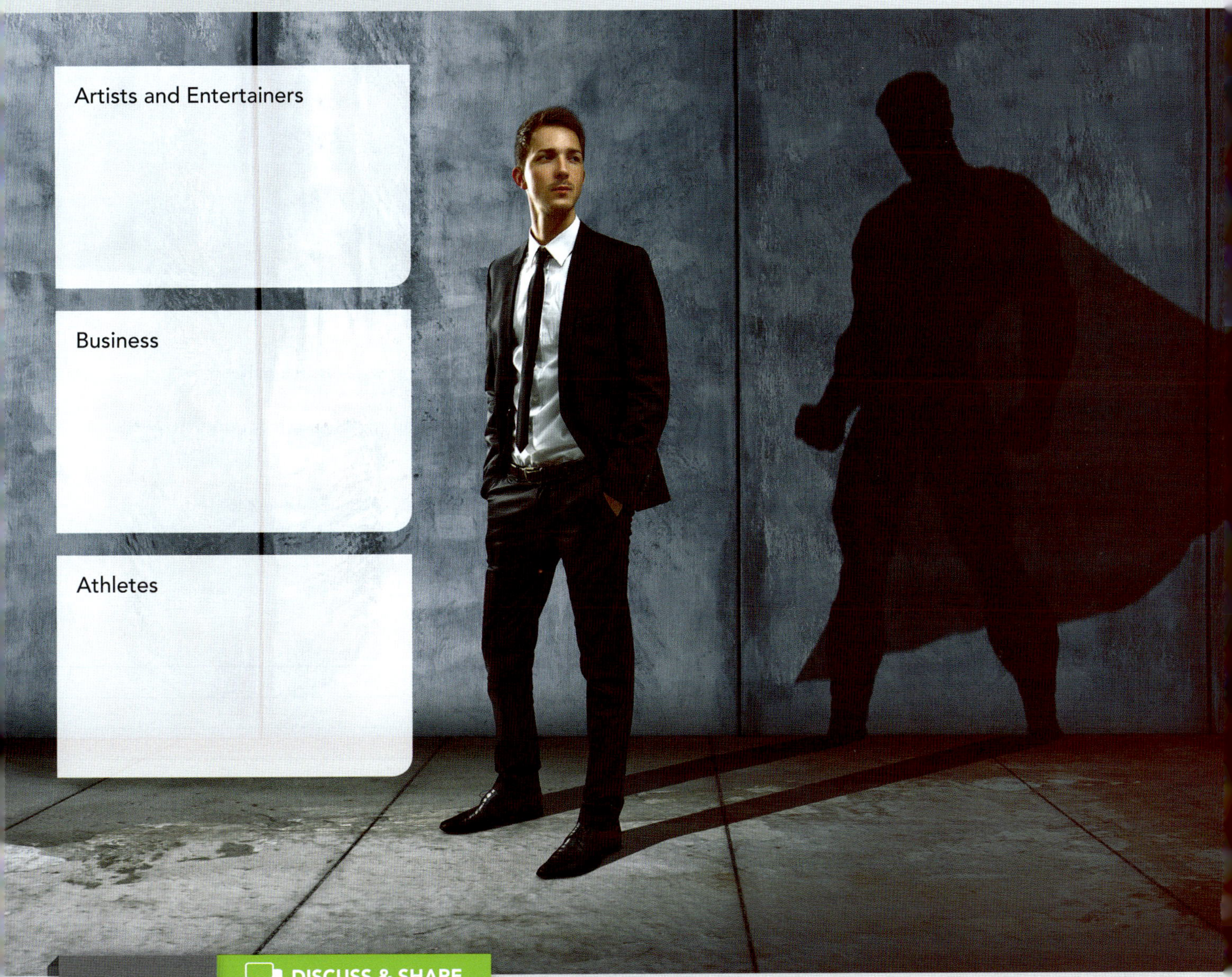

Artists and Entertainers

Business

Athletes

VIDEO

DISCUSS & SHARE

3 **IN GROUPS** **Watch the video and answer the question.**

SYM Is being famous the same as being extraordinary?

In this unit, you will ...

- talk about a role model, describe a memorable event, and tell an anecdote.
- use thinking skills: evaluate, analyze, and understand.
- read a biography.
- use strategies to speculate about reasons, sequence events, use words you know when you don't know an exact word.
- use communication skills to give a short speech for a citizen award.
- learn strategies for using personal experience in writing.

READING

A Do you have any role models? Why do you admire them?

B 1.01 READING SKILL—Skim a text Look at the text quickly for one minute. Don't try to read every word. Then close your book and note down any information you remember.

LILA DOWNS

My role model is Lila Downs. She was born in Oaxaca, Mexico, in 1968. She is a Mexican-American singer-songwriter and actress. At the age of eight, she started singing mariachi songs. She became a professional singer when she was at school. Her family **emigrated** from Mexico to the US when she was 14. While they were living there, her father died. After that, Lila and her mother moved back to Mexico.

While she was working in her mother's store, she met her future husband, the musician Paul Cohen. He had a business in the US, so Lila moved from Oaxaca to Minnesota. She went to the University of Minnesota. While she was studying there, she started a music group called La Trova Serrana. It was very **successful**, and Lila decided to leave school to **focus on** music. Lila had a small **role** in the movie *Frida* and worked on the music for the movie *Like Water for Chocolate*. Here are three things you probably don't know about Lila:

- In 2010, while she was traveling the world on her Black Magic Woman Tour, she **revealed** that she had an adopted son named Benito Dxuladi.
- In 2014, scientists named an **insect** after her. The *Liladownsia fraile* is a very colorful grasshopper. They named it after her because Lila often wears colorful, traditional clothes.
- She sings in Spanish, English, and her native language of Mixtec.

I really **look up to** Lila Downs because she looks for ways to **improve** people's lives through music. I'd love to meet her and ask her this question: "What were you singing about in the song 'Shake Away'?"

C Scan the article in B and answer the questions.

1 Where is Lila from? ____________
2 How old was Lila when she moved to the US? ____________
3 When did Lila reveal that she had adopted her son? ____________
4 What type of animal did scientists name after Lila? ____________
5 What languages does Lila sing in? ____________

D Read the article in B in detail to check your answers.

E THINKING SKILL—Evaluate Is it important to have role models? Are most famous people good role models? Discuss and give examples.

VOCABULARY

A Match the bold words from the text in READING B to the definitions.

1 ____________: left your country to move to a different country (verb)
2 ____________: admire; think someone is a good role model (phrasal verb)
3 ____________: make something better (verb)
4 ____________: told a secret (verb)
5 ____________: a small animal with six legs and wings (noun)
6 ____________: achieving wealth, admiration, or popularity (adjective)
7 ____________: pay attention to; concentrate on (phrasal verb)
8 ____________: a part in a movie or a play (noun)

MAKE IT YOURS

Choose a famous role model that you look up to. Find an article about his or her life. Write down any interesting facts that you find in the article.

GRAMMAR past progressive

A Underline the past progressive verb forms in READING B.

While they were living there, her father died.

B Complete the rules with words from the box.

–ing were continued was

1 The past progressive describes actions that began in the past and ______________ for some time.
2 The past progressive always includes the form ______________ or ______________.
3 In the past progressive, add ______________ to the base form of the verb.

For more practice, go to page 142.

C Complete the conversation with the past progressive form of the verb in parentheses.

Ben: I called you last night, but you didn't answer. What **1** ______________ (you do)?
Ashley: We **2** ______________ (celebrate) my great-grandfather's 100th birthday.
Ben: Really? One hundred! That's amazing. Was he your role model while you **3** ______________ (grow) up?
Ashley: Yes, definitely. He was my hero! He **4** ______________ (open) presents when you called. Everyone **5** ______________ (clap).
Ben: I'm sure he had a great time yesterday.
Ashley: I think so. We **6** ______________ (not plan) for the party to end at midnight!

D IN PAIRS Ask and answer the questions.

1 What were you doing …
a in the summer? **b** in 2016? **c** last Thursday? **d** last night?

A: What were you doing last night? *B: I was visiting my grandparents.*

SPEAKING

A Read about Ann Makosinski, a young inventor and role model. Why is she famous?

Ann Makosinski
1997—born October 3, Canada
2011—in Philippines, her friend fails exam because there's no electricity at night
2011—Ann gets idea for flashlight
2012—develops flashlight powered by body heat

B IN PAIRS Discuss the events in Ann's life using information from the notes.

C IN GROUPS Discuss how you think Ann's flashlight works. Use the Confident Communicator box to help you.

CONFIDENT COMMUNICATOR
START TALKING

Use the following expressions to talk about something you are not 100% sure about:
I'm not sure, but I think it may/could be …
Maybe it works without …
Perhaps/Maybe you can use it …

VOCABULARY reactions

A Match the sentences (1–6) to the pictures (a–f). Write the letter.

1 Were you **disappointed** that you didn't get a good grade? _____
2 Walt's phone rang in the middle of the night. He was **worried**. _____
3 There was a snake crossing the path. I was so **scared**. I'm afraid of snakes! _____
4 I won a free trip around the world. I'm **thrilled**! _____
5 I was **glad** the bus came. It was raining very heavily. _____
6 I'm **confused**! Which way do I go? _____

LISTENING

A 1.02 LISTENING SKILL—Listen for specific information **Listen to four people talk about memorable events. Match the speakers (1–4) to how they felt (a–d).**

1 Katrin: _____	a thrilled
2 Giovanni: _____	b glad
3 Kyle: _____	c worried
4 Gemma: _____	d confused

B THINKING SKILL—Analyze **Why do you think the speakers felt the way they did? Evaluate if you would feel the same way.**

I think Katrin was worried because she loves animals. I would feel …

PRONUNCIATION vowel + consonant + e

A 1.03 **Listen and notice the change in the vowel sounds. The –*e* changes the vowel to a long sound.**

Suddenly, a police officer shouted, "**Hide**!"
We **hid** in a café.

B 1.04 **Practice saying the words. Listen and check your pronunciation.**

1 hid hide **2** at ate **3** mad made **4** rid ride

GRAMMAR past progressive vs. simple past

A Underline the action in progress and circle the action that interrupts it.

1 I was watching the game at my friend's house when the phone rang.

2 I was working for NASA on the Mars mission when it happened.

3 My boss called me in the middle of the night while I was sleeping.

4 When the plane came down, we were staying in a hotel.

B Choose the correct option to complete the grammar rules.

1 The past progressive describes an **interrupting action** / **action in progress**.
2 The simple past describes the **interrupting action** / **action in progress**.
3 We use ***when*** / ***while*** to introduce the action in progress.
4 We use ***when*** / ***while*** to introduce the interrupting action.
5 We use a comma after *when* and *while* clauses at the **beginning** / **end** of a sentence.

For more practice, go to page 142.

C Complete the text with the correct form of the verb in parentheses. Use the past progressive or the past simple.

Kiera: Did you hear that news story about the animal rescue?
Asha: No. What **1** ____________ (happen)?
Kiera: I **2** ____________ (read) about it on the way to work yesterday. Well, you know there was that hurricane in Texas? Hurricane Harvey, I think it was.
Asha: Yes, I remember it.
Kiera: Well, after the hurricane, when people **3** ____________ (leave) their homes, there were lots of pets that **4** ____________ (live) on the streets. The animal rescue centers had no room for them. So, an airline organized a flight to take about 60 of the animals from Houston to San Diego to find new forever homes! I **5** ____________ (cry) when I read the story. There was a photo of the pilot and he **6** ____________ (hold) some of the puppies. They were so cute!
Asha: The perfect happy ending, huh?

D IN PAIRS What happened on your way to class today? Describe the actions in progress and interrupting actions.

A: While I was walking to class today, I saw my friend Gabriel.

B: My phone rang while I was getting on the bus.

SPEAKING

A Think about a memorable event in your life. Make notes about:

- what happened
- where you were
- when it happened
- what you were doing
- how you felt

B IN GROUPS Take turns describing the events. Ask questions about the details. Use the Confident Communicator box to help you.

A: I remember the storm in 2016. I was living in Monterrey at the time. It started raining while I was walking to work.

B: Were you scared?

CONFIDENT COMMUNICATOR
REPAIR IT

If you don't know a word in English, here are some things you can do:
Use a word that means something similar (e.g., *very worried* for *scared*).
Give a short description of the event (e.g., *a lot of rain* for *storm*).

Coincidences

VOCABULARY family situations

A Match the words and phrases from the box to the pictures (1–8).

adopted divorced engaged large family only child single single parent twins

1 
______

2 
______

3 
______

4 
______

5 
______

6 
______

7 
______

8 
______

B Complete the sentences with the words and phrases from A.

1 My sister and I are ______. She was born 10 minutes before I was. We look the same, but we are different.
2 Jack comes from a ______. He has eight brothers and sisters.
3 I am ______, but I want to get married in the future.
4 I am an ______. When I was growing up, I wanted a brother or sister.
5 My parents are ______. My mom got married again last year.
6 Dan is a/an ______. His wife died about five years ago, so he takes care of his kids on his own.
7 We got ______ last year. We're getting married this summer.
8 Lois's parents ______ her when she was six weeks old.

C IN PAIRS Discuss your family. Ask questions to find out more information.

LISTENING

A Look at the picture. What do you notice about the people?

B 1.05 LISTENING SKILL—Predict the story
Listen to the first half of an anecdote about an amazing coincidence. What do you think will happen next?

C 1.06 Listen to the second half of the anecdote to check. Were you correct?

D 1.07 **Now listen to the whole anecdote. Circle the sequencing phrases you hear.**

about two years ago	about a month after that	the next day
about six months ago	about three months later	a few days later
a week later	later that day	finally
a month later	later on	in the end

E THINKING SKILL—Understand What was the coincidence in this anecdote? Summarize.

MAKE IT REAL

To show you are surprised about something in an anecdote or story, you can say:

You're kidding! *That's unbelievable!* *No way!*

WRITING

A Read this anecdote about an amazing coincidence. What do you think is interesting about it?

This is an anecdote a friend told me. It's about a woman who was adopted at six months old. One day, she was in the hair salon in the new neighborhood she was living in, when she saw a woman who looked similar to her. They talked a little bit about their lives. The young woman said she was adopted as a baby.

"When's your birthday?" asked the older woman.

"January 25, 1998," said the young woman. The older woman was shocked.

"I gave a daughter up for adoption. She was born on January 25, 1998," she said.

After that, they both took a DNA test and discovered they were mother and daughter. They were so glad to find one another. I think this story is interesting because it is an amazing coincidence.

B Think of an interesting anecdote that happened to you or someone you know. Make notes about the following:

- who the anecdote involves
- what happened
- where it happened
- what the people were doing
- how they felt
- why you think the anecdote is interesting

C Write the main events of your anecdote.

____

____

____

D Write your anecdote in your notebook. Make sure that the events are in the correct order.

E IN PAIRS Share your writing. What was interesting about your partner's anecdote?

SPEAKING

A Think of an interesting anecdote you read in a book, heard on the news, or saw on TV.

B IN GROUPS Share your anecdotes. Decide on the anecdote that you all like. Use the Confident Communicator box to help you.

CONFIDENT COMMUNICATOR
START TALKING

Use sequencing words and phrases to connect the events in an anecdote.
About three months ago … / Two weeks ago … / Last week …
After that … / Then …
In the end … / Finally …

Language and Life

Communication – Citizen Award

A What is a hero? Do you know of any heroes in your community?

B 1.08 Read the magazine article about heroes. Then choose *True* or *False*.

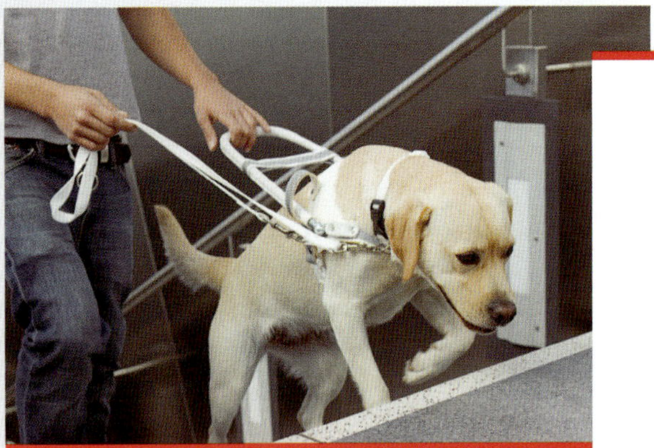

Victor Karlsson

Meet 20-year-old Victor Karlsson from Malmo, Sweden. When Victor was eight years old, he became blind in an accident. With help from his family and friends, Victor is now a local hero in Malmo. Victor and his guide dog Charlie are helping improve the lives of blind children and adults by raising money. In 2018, Victor raised 1,500 euros walking 111 km between Malmo and Copenhagen. In 2020, he is planning to run a half-marathon. "Everyone looks up to Victor," says his friend Katya. "He's a true role model."

Petra Gonzalez

Nineteen-year-old Petra Gonzalez saved her sister from a fire in their home in Mexico. Petra, a university student, woke up one night to the smell of smoke. She woke up her sister. She was carrying her sister out of their apartment when she saw the fire on the other side of the house. Amazingly, firefighters arrived in time to save both girls. Petra got an award from the local mayor. "I was really scared," said Petra, "but I was just doing what any sister would do."

Mimi Kallas

While Mimi Kallas was working in a tourist office in her home town in Greece, she noticed men and women on the streets asking for food. Mimi stopped working at her job and started a food service for homeless people. She collects extra food from stores and cooks up to 100 meals a day in the kitchen of a school. She gives out the food for free to anyone who needs it. "Without Mimi, we couldn't survive," said one man. "She is an amazing woman. I'm so glad she is here to help us."

1 Victor was eight when he went blind. True / False
2 Victor ran a half-marathon in 2018. True / False
3 Petra is an only child. True / False
4 The fire was in Petra's school. True / False
5 Mimi works in a tourist office. True / False
6 Mimi cooks food for people at a school. True / False

C IN PAIRS Discuss why each person from B is a hero. Give reasons.

A: Who do you think is the most heroic?
B: I think … is the most heroic because …
A: Oh, really? I think … is the most heroic because …

D IN GROUPS Imagine you work for a local community committee. You want to offer a Citizen Award to a person who did something extraordinary. Research news websites online to find examples of heroic acts and write a list.

This woman in Sao Paulo is a hero. She saved a child's life.

E IN GROUPS Role-play an awards ceremony where the heroes are given their awards and make short thank-you speeches.

A: Please welcome …, who gets a Citizen Award today for helping out every week at the local baseball club …
B: I'd like to say how thrilled I am to get this award. I love helping out at the local baseball club because …

F Discuss the questions.

1 Did you clearly communicate the reasons for giving the award? Why or why not?
2 In what other situations does a group of people decide who wins an award?

MAKE IT DIGITAL

Go online and find examples of heroic acts in your country. Talk about which ones you think are extraordinary and why.

VOCABULARY review

SCORE: / 10

A Choose the correct option.

1 Raul was **glad** / **disappointed** when he got bad grades in his final exams.
2 Were you **scared** / **thrilled** when you heard a hurricane was coming?
3 Please don't talk to me while I'm studying, or I will get **glad** / **confused**.
4 I'm a little **worried** / **disappointed** about tomorrow's party. What will happen if people don't come?
5 My parents were **scared** / **thrilled** when I told them I got an award.
6 Jackson **is** / **isn't** an only child. He has a brother named Harrison.
7 Dad comes from a **large** / **small** family. He has five brothers and two sisters.
8 Pavlos and Christina got **adopted** / **divorced**. Pavlos is getting married again next month.
9 My parents got **engaged** / **adopted** when they were in their 30s.
10 I'm **an only parent** / **a single parent**, but the kids see their dad on the weekends.

GRAMMAR review

SCORE: / 10

A Correct the errors and rewrite the sentences.

1 What you were doing last New Year's Eve? ______
2 In 2016, I living in Mexico City. ______
3 At noon, my friends and I were eat lunch. ______
4 My brother were making breakfast this morning. ______
5 They was watching a movie last night. ______

B Unscramble and write.

1 started raining / While / was / for the bus, / it / waiting / I ______
2 while / The movie / our tickets / started / we / buying / were ______
3 rang / was / I / my phone / working / when ______
4 swimming / We / were / when / happened / the accident ______
5 got / watching TV / The kids / when / home / were / their father ______

16–20 correct: You can discuss family situations and reactions. You can use the past progressive.
0–15 correct: Look again at the Vocabulary and Grammar sections in the unit.

TOTAL SCORE: / 20

WHAT DO YOU KNOW NOW? Look back at page 7 and add words you know now to the boxes.

STUDY SKILLS USING PERSONAL EXPERIENCE

Take the quiz. Then go to **Study Skills** on page 127.
Find the answers and learn more about using personal experience.

1 Which two of the following things do we usually find in personal narratives?
a evidence **b** feelings **c** descriptions

2 Personal narratives are usually subjective.
a True **b** False

3 Which two of the following things do we usually find in factual accounts?
a chronological events **b** numbers and statistics **c** use of the word *I*

UNIT 2

Party!

WHAT DO YOU ALREADY KNOW?

1 Think about occasions you celebrate. Write the words.

2 IN PAIRS Share and compare your ideas. Think of more words to add to each category.

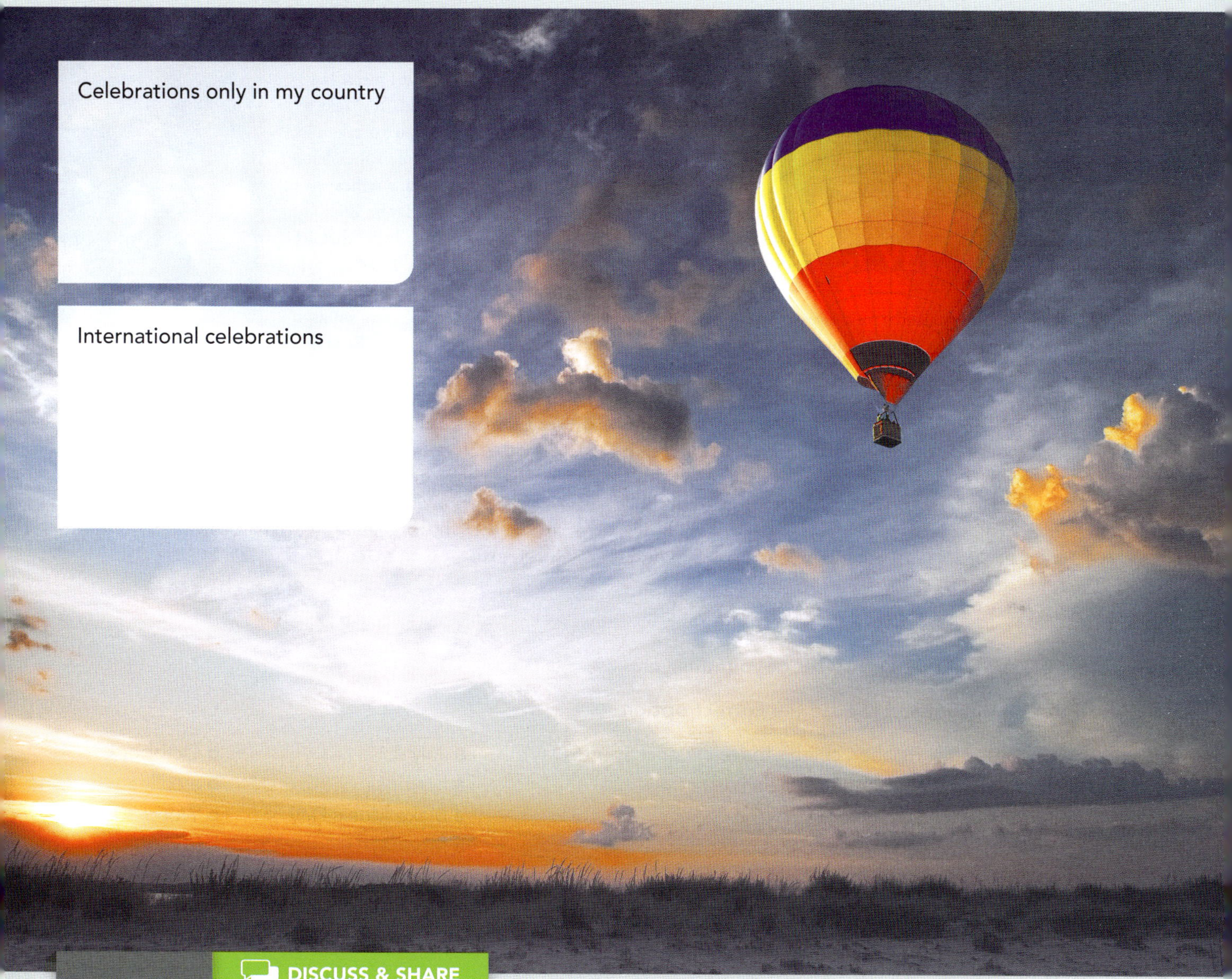

Celebrations only in my country

International celebrations

DISCUSS & SHARE

VIDEO

3 IN GROUPS Watch the video and answer the question.

SYM Do you prefer to buy gifts or buy experiences for celebrations?

In this unit, you will ...

- talk about official and unofficial holidays, spending habits, and celebrations.
- use thinking skills: analyze and evaluate.
- read about unusual holidays.
- use strategies to start and keep talking by giving reasons, giving opinions, and asking follow-up questions.
- use creativity skills to work with others and create your own graduation ceremony.
- follow a hotel manager to learn about the jobs and skills needed in the hospitality industry.

Days of the Year

READING

A **Look at the pictures in B. What are the people doing?**

B **READING SKILL—Predict the topic** **Read the title and look at the pictures. What do you think you are going to read about? Check (✓) one of the ideas.**

- ☐ a story about someone's birthday
- ☐ a blog about celebrations around the world
- ☐ an article about celebrating unusual days of the year

EVERY DAY *is a* HOLIDAY!

Take a look at your **calendar** for the year ahead. Some dates show an **official** event that people **celebrate** somewhere in the world. For example, Americans celebrate Independence Day on July 4. On October 8, the Japanese celebrate Health and Sports Day. A lot of people **get the day off** work, and schools and businesses are closed. People may eat special food on these days or give and **receive** gifts.

Then, there are unofficial holidays. These are days when people sometimes **arrange** a party at school or at work. Unofficial holidays celebrate unimportant and fun things like food, movies, books, and TV shows.

To show you what I mean, last week, a **colleague** said, "It's 'Take a Selfie Day'! Today you can take a lot of selfies." In my opinion, there's too much time spent taking selfies—you don't need a special day for it!

There are a few websites that list all these celebrations. Think of any day of the year, and there is something to celebrate. I learned there are days of the year for everything: Read in the Bathtub Day (February 9), World Yoga Day (February 22), and my favorite, Make Music Day (June 21). A lot of days celebrate food, like Caesar Salad Day on July 4 and Eat a Peach Day on August 22. There are too many dates for me to remember!

I am thinking of asking my **boss** if I can get the day off on the second Friday of March. It's World Sleep Day. And a little advice for you—don't think of asking me to do anything on Lazy Day (August 10)!

C 2.01 **Read the text in B to check your answer.**

D **Read the text again and choose the correct option.**

1	When do people in Japan celebrate Health and Sports Day?	**a** July 4	**b** October 8
2	Who told the writer about Take a Selfie Day?	**a** her boss	**b** a colleague
3	What is the writer's favorite Day of the Year?	**a** Make Music Day	**b** World Yoga Day
4	What day of the week is World Sleep Day on?	**a** Monday	**b** Friday

E **THINKING SKILL—Analyze** **What holidays are celebrated in your country but not in other countries?**

VOCABULARY

A **Match the bold words from the text in READING B to the definitions.**

1. agreed upon or arranged by people in power (adjective) ______
2. a chart with days of the year showing seasonal information (noun) ______
3. when you don't have to go to work or school (phrase) ______
4. do something to recognize an important or special event (verb) ______
5. a person who is in charge at work (noun) ______
6. make plans for an event (verb) ______
7. get something from someone (verb) ______
8. a person you work with (noun) ______

MAKE IT YOURS

Search online for "days of the year" and find more fun holidays. Select a day and share it with your classmates.

GRAMMAR quantifiers

A **Look back at the text in READING B. Circle these words: *some, a lot of, a little, too many, any, too much, a few.* Underline the noun that follows. Write the phrases in the correct column.**

Countable	Uncountable
some dates	

B **Choose the correct option to complete the grammar rules.**

1 Use *some* with countable nouns / uncountable nouns / both.
2 Use *a lot of* with countable nouns / uncountable nouns / both.
3 Use *a little* with countable nouns / uncountable nouns / both.
4 Use *too many* with countable nouns / uncountable nouns / both.
5 Use *any* with countable nouns / uncountable nouns / both.
6 Use *too much* with countable nouns / uncountable nouns / both.
7 Use *a few* with countable nouns / uncountable nouns / both.

For more practice, go to page 143.

C **Choose the correct quantifier.**

Pasteles de hoja are a popular dish in Puerto Rico, but they are also made in the Dominican Republic, Colombia, and El Salvador. They are usually made around Christmas and families often spend **1 a little / a few** days preparing them. It's common to make **2 a lot of / a few** pasteles at the same time (usually between 50 and 200!). Here is the basic recipe: Make a vegetable dough from green banana flour. Fill the dough with **3 some / a few** meat. Don't add **4 too many / too much** meat because you have to add the chickpeas, raisins, and olives, too. Wrap the pasteles in banana leaves and steam them. People usually freeze some of them to enjoy on Three Kings Day on January 6. Or they take **5 a little / some** boxes of pasteles as a gift to family or friends. They are delicious, but very big, so you may not want to eat **6 too much / too many**!

D **IN PAIRS Think about a celebration that you went to recently that had food and drinks. What did you have? Discuss. Use quantifiers where necessary.**

I went to a party for my colleague's birthday. There was a lot of food. I had a few sandwiches and some salad.

SPEAKING

A **March 26 is Make Up Your Own Holiday Day. On this day you can choose to celebrate anything you like. Think about what you would like to celebrate on this holiday. Make notes about:**

- the name of your holiday
- what you do to celebrate it
- where you want to celebrate
- why you want to celebrate it

B **IN GROUPS Share your ideas about your own holiday. Use the Confident Communicator box to help you. Whose ideas do you like best? Why?**

CONFIDENT COMMUNICATOR
KEEP TALKING

Use *because* and *because of* to give reasons.
Because + subject + verb
I'd like to make a holiday for pets ***because I think*** *…*
Because of + noun
I probably won't celebrate the day at the beach ***because of the weather****. It's too hot.*

LESSON 2 The Business of Holidays

VOCABULARY money and shopping

A Match the underlined phrases (1–6) to the definitions (a–f). Write the letter.

1 I love traveling, so I usually spend money on trips abroad. ____
2 You can make money by selling handmade gifts online. ____
3 I don't like to lend money to friends. ____
4 I never waste money on things I don't need. ____
5 It's easy to overspend at certain times of the year. I spend too much money at Thanksgiving. ____
6 Sometimes I borrow money from my parents, but I always pay it back. ____

a get money by working or selling something
b ask someone to give you money because you don't have enough
c buy things you don't need
d buy something
e give someone money because they don't have enough
f spend more money than you have

MAKE IT REAL

There are many informal synonyms for money in English. Here are a few: *cash, bucks, loot, bread, dough, capital.*

B Choose the correct option to complete the text.

Are you looking for extra ways to **1** make / spend money? Instead of **2** borrowing / lending money from a friend or member of your family, here are a few simple ideas to help:

- Don't **3** waste / lend money on expensive gifts when, with a little imagination, you can make your own. How about making cookies and giving them as gifts to family and friends?
- Many stores have sales in January. It's easy to find things at good prices at this time of year. Buy the items you need to make your card and gifts. Decide how much you can afford so you don't **4** waste / overspend.

C IN PAIRS Ask and answer questions using the phrases in A.

A: Do you lend money to friends? *B: Sometimes, if they really need it.*

LISTENING

A 2.02 LISTENING SKILL—Identify opinions Listen to a conversation in a store. Do you think the man and woman agree or disagree with one another?

B Write the phrases under the correct headings.

Exactly. I know. That's true. You're right. I disagree. I'm not sure about that. Yeah!

Phrases for agreeing

____ ____
____ ____
____

Phrases for disagreeing

____ ____

C THINKING SKILL—Evaluate Do you agree or disagree that you should never borrow or lend money? Why or why not?

GRAMMAR enough / not enough

A Decide if the nouns that follow *enough* and *not enough* are *Countable* or *Uncountable*.

1 Not enough people shop around these days. ____________

2 They don't have enough money. ____________

3 I have enough decorations. ____________

B Choose the correct option to complete the rules.

1 *Enough* shows that the amount is **the right amount** / **not the right amount**.

2 *Not enough* shows that the amount is **the right amount** / **not the right amount**.

3 *Enough* and *not enough* are used with **countable nouns** / **uncountable nouns** / **both**.

For more practice, go to page 144.

C Look at the pictures and write sentences with *enough* or *not enough*.

1

2

3

4

1 I / have enough / money / buy / this hat.

____

2 There / be enough / eggs / make / the cake.

____

3 She / have enough / food / on her plate.

____

4 He / have enough / casual / shoes.

____

D IN PAIRS Do you think there are enough national celebrations throughout the year in your country? Discuss the days in the year when people get the day off.

SPEAKING

A Do you think some people spend a lot of money on celebrations these days? On which celebrations?

B IN PAIRS Discuss your opinions about what people spend money on for different celebrations. Use the Confident Communicator box to help you.

CONFIDENT COMMUNICATOR
START TALKING

Use informal or formal language depending on your situation.

Informal
I think people waste money on decorations for holidays.
I don't think it's a good idea to borrow money for celebrations.
I bet some people spend lots of money on gifts.
I guess lending money to a friend is OK.

More formal
In my opinion, people shouldn't feel they have to buy gifts.
From my point of view, Independence Day is an important celebration.

LESSON 3 Celebration Food and Drink

VOCABULARY food and drink packaging

A Label the food items in the pictures (1–8) with words from the box.

bag of orangesbottle of water	box of chocolatescan of nuts	carton of juicejar of olives	jug of apple cider package of cookies

1

____

2

____

3

____

4

____

5

____

6

____

7

____

8

____

B IN PAIRS What do you usually give or receive as a gift on holidays? Discuss.

A: I usually make cookies and give a box to my friends at Christmas.

B: I get a jar of honey from my aunt. She keeps bees.

LISTENING

A 2.03 You are going to listen to a chef describing food he is making for a special celebration. Listen to the introduction and choose the celebration he is talking about.

1 St. Patrick's Day **2** Thanksgiving **3** Chinese New Year **4** International Women's Day

B 2.04 LISTENING SKILL—Listen for specific information Listen to the recipe and complete each ingredient with one word.

Dumplings (makes about 30)

2 ______________ of dumpling wrappers

1 can of water chestnuts

1 ______________ of green onions

2 boxes of mushrooms

2 teaspoons of Chinese spices

garlic

small ______________ of oil

For the dipping sauce:

1 ______________ of sweet chili sauce

ginger

sesame seeds

1/2 ______________ of soy sauce

C IN PAIRS Think about a celebration food that you like. Make a note of the ingredients you need and discuss.

A: I really love pavlova.

B: What do you need to make it?

A: You need a carton of eggs, a carton of cream, and …

D THINKING SKILL—Evaluate Which celebration food or drink from your country would you recommend to a foreign visitor? Why?

PRONUNCIATION /tʃ/ and /ʃ/

A 2.05 Listen. Notice the difference between the /tʃ/ sound and the /ʃ/ sound.

1 shop chop **2** ships chips **3** sheep cheap

B 2.05 Listen again and repeat. Exaggerate the /tʃ/ *and* /ʃ/ sounds as you say the words.

C IN PAIRS Practice saying the pairs of words. Can your partner hear the difference between the /tʃ/ *and* /ʃ/ sounds when you say the words?

WRITING

A Read the paragraph describing a celebration. What does the festival celebrate? Do you have a celebration like this in your country?

We celebrate Grand Kadooment Day at the end of the Crop Over festival. A lot of people in the Caribbean celebrate it, too, **but** it's the national celebration of Barbados. In the past, Crop Over was a celebration to mark the end of the sugar cane season. People dress up in costumes or in their best clothes, **and** there are street parades and street food festivals all over the island. We normally eat fried fish **or** fish cakes and sno-cones—ice with flavors such as ginger or coconut. I really like it **because** it's a holiday. We get the day off work, **so** we can have some family time.

B Match the bold linking words in A to their use.

1 ____________: introduces a contrasting idea
2 ____________: adds extra information
3 ____________: gives a reason
4 ____________: gives a result
5 ____________: gives an alternative

C In your notebook, write a short paragraph about a celebration you like. Use linking words to connect your sentences.

SPEAKING

A Imagine you are ordering a food gift box online for a friend who lives abroad. You want to add some special celebration foods that are typical of your country. Make a list of the items you would include.

B IN PAIRS Show your list to your partner. Add any items from your partner's list that you would like to include. Use the Confident Communicator box to help you.

C IN GROUPS Share your ideas with the members of your group. Decide whose gift box you would most like to receive. Explain why.

CONFIDENT COMMUNICATOR
KEEP TALKING

You can use *Did you* to ask follow-up questions in a conversation. For example:
Did you include a jar of …?
No! I forgot. But I should. I included a box of … Did you?
Yes, I did. You can't celebrate … without those!

Language and Life

Creativity – Graduation Celebrations

A 2.06 **Read an article about different graduation celebrations from around the world. Then choose *Yes* or *No*.**

Graduation Ceremonies Around the **World**

Sweden
Swedish graduates wear sailor's caps to their graduation ceremony. The ceremony usually starts with singing. Parents arrive and give their children gifts tied with ribbons, and the graduates wear the ribbons around their necks. At the end of the ceremony, there is a parade through the streets of the town, and local people come to congratulate the students.

Japan
In Japan, graduation happens in March, before the new school year. High school students wear their school uniforms for their graduation ceremony. If their school doesn't have a uniform, they wear formal clothes, such as a suit for men and a kimono for women. The principal usually gives a speech. Then, the student president gives a speech.

United States
In the US, it's common for a famous person (sometimes a graduate of the university) or a politician to give a speech to congratulate the graduates. In some large American universities, the ceremony happens in a sports stadium. Students normally wear special caps and gowns in the colors of their university or department.

South Africa
Graduates from the University of Witwatersrand in Johannesburg have an interesting musical tradition. The graduation ceremony there starts with a formal procession by the teachers and workers at the university. After that, they play the song "I Got You (I Feel Good)" by James Brown for the students to dance to.

Argentina
Students in Argentina usually wear old clothes for their graduation ceremony. The reason? Family and friends throw sticky or messy food at the graduates, like flour, eggs, ketchup, and soda. It's supposed to bring them good luck!

1 Graduates in Sweden wear traditional caps and gowns. Yes / No
2 Graduation ceremonies in Japan happen at the end of the year. Yes / No
3 In Argentina, graduates wear formal clothes. Yes / No
4 One university in South Africa plays a particular song at graduation. Yes / No
5 In the US, graduation ceremonies often happen in large outdoor spaces. Yes / No

B **Which graduation ceremony described in A would you like to go to? Why?**

C **IN PAIRS Discuss some of the things that people do in your country to celebrate high school or university graduation. Use the prompts to help you.**

- have a family meal
- celebrate with a night out with friends
- go on vacation with classmates
- have a party at home
- go to a formal organized event
- other: ______________________

A: People usually celebrate by going to a formal organized event at a hotel or club.

B: Yes, they do. But sometimes they go on vacation with their classmates. We went to …

D **IN GROUPS Imagine you are on the Student Committee at your university. Read the email from the university president and brainstorm ideas for your ideal graduation ceremony.**

New Message

From: johnwilson@university.uni

To: studentcommittee@university.uni Cc Bcc

Subject: RE: Graduation Speakers

Dear Student Committee members,

As you may know, we are looking for speakers for next year's graduation ceremony. We would like your help in choosing one or two public figures who our graduating students respect and admire. We would also like your thoughts on the following things for the ceremony:

- what students should wear
- where the ceremony should take place
- which students should give a speech
- what music you think should be played

We look forward to your ideas.

Please present your ideas to me at our next meeting on March 15.

Regards,

John Wilson
University President

Send

E **Make a list of one or two suggestions for each of the points in the university president's email.**

____

____

____

____

F **Give a presentation to the class and the university president (your teacher). Which ideas for a graduation ceremony do most people like? Take a vote.**

G **Discuss the questions.**

1 Was it easy or hard to work together to think of creative ideas?
2 In what other situations do you listen to different people offer creative ideas?

MAKE IT DIGITAL

Go online and watch videos of graduation ceremonies from around the world. Which ones do you think you would like to go to?

VOCABULARY review

SCORE: / 10

A Complete the sentences with the words from the box.

bag boxes can jar package

1 How many ____________ of breakfast cereal do you buy a month?
2 I ate nearly a whole ____________ of chocolate cookies!
3 Dad bought my mom a ____________ of marmalade when he went to Spain.
4 I'd rather get a ____________ of potato chips than a box of raisins for my snack.
5 Do you want to get a ____________ of tomato soup or a bag of tomatoes?

B Choose the best option.

It's easy to **1 overspend / waste** at holidays. I try to **2 borrow / save** some money every week so that I can buy little gifts for everyone in my family. My dad loves chocolate, so I often get him a **3 box / can** of Swiss chocolates. My mom loves scarves, so I shop **4 around / about** to find her pretty ones. My sister's easy to buy for. I usually get her a **5 jug / bottle** of perfume. And then, there's the dog. He always gets a toy!

GRAMMAR review

SCORE: / 10

A Choose the correct option.

1 **A few / lot of** people came to the office party. There were only about 20 people there.
2 This coffee has too **much / many** sugar in it. I can't drink it.
3 **Some / A little** people go to their graduation ceremony in formal clothes!
4 I don't think there are **a little / enough** public holidays in my country.
5 The party dress was too **much / many** money for me to buy.

B Complete the text with the words and phrases from the box.

a few a lot enough some too many

One country with **1** ____________ of public holidays is Argentina. In total, there are 19 public holidays. **2** ____________ people say that 19 holidays is **3** ____________. Others say that holidays help people relax and that, in general, people don't have **4** ____________ time off work. **5** ____________ countries have a similar number; Colombia has 18 days and Thailand has 16 days.

16–20 correct: You can discuss money, shopping, and food and drink packaging. You can use quantifiers to talk about *enough / not enough*.
0–15 correct: Look again at the Vocabulary and Grammar sections in the unit.

TOTAL SCORE: / 20

WHAT DO YOU KNOW NOW? Look back at page 17 and add the words you know now to the boxes.

FOLLOW A PRO HOSPITALITY

Take the quiz about hospitality. Then go to **Follow A Pro** on page 128. Find the answers and learn more about the hospitality industry.

1 When did the world's oldest hotel, located in Japan, open?
a 705 **b** 1205 **c** 1505

2 What country gets the most international tourists per year?
a the US **b** China **c** France

3 How many hotel rooms are there in the world (in millions)?
a 5.1 **b** 8.5 **c** 17.2

UNIT 3

What's Trending?

WHAT DO YOU ALREADY KNOW?

1 **Think of TV shows, movies, and music you like. Make a list.**

2 IN PAIRS **Share and compare your favorites. Add more things to your lists.**

TV shows

Movies

Music

DISCUSS & SHARE

VIDEO

3 IN GROUPS **Watch the video and answer the question.**

SYM Do you prefer to watch entertainment at home or in public?

In this unit, you will ...

- talk about entertainers in your area, the music industry, and your viewing habits.
- use thinking skills: understand and evaluate.
- read about street performers.
- use strategies to start and keep talking by making notes, asking for opinions, and using qualifying phrases.
- use decision-making skills to plan an event to save a theater.
- design questionnaires for research.

READING

A **Look at the pictures in the article in B. Which street entertainer do you think is the most talented?**

B **3.01 READING SKILL—Identify main ideas Read the magazine article about street entertainers around the world. Then write 1–2 sentences for each entertainer. Explain what they do.**

Street Entertainers From Around the WORLD

Juan Eze is a street entertainer from Buenos Aires. "Everywhere I go, people always ask me what my **trick** is," he says, "but I never tell anyone the secret of my act. Nobody knows." Juan sits for up to four hours at a time without moving, but he says he doesn't get bored. What's amazing is that he looks like he's **floating.** "Everyone thinks I'm doing nothing, but I'm actually watching everything around me."

Marcel Debard, a fire-eater and acrobat, works on the streets of Casablanca. "I started **performing** about 15 years ago in a circus in Paris. Then, someone asked me to help with the fire-eating act and I started to learn how to do it. Is it dangerous? Well, yes, but it's more **dangerous** for the audience. We have to make sure nobody gets hurt. That's why we **blow** the **fire** over the heads of the people."

Huang Jun does a **puppet** show on the streets of Yangzhou, China. "Puppets are popular forms of entertainment in China, for adults and kids," he explains. "In most puppet shows around the world, no one sees the person **controlling** the puppets. In Chinese puppet shows, everybody can see everything. It's part of the entertainment—to see how we make the puppets move."

C **Read the article in B again. Match the questions (1–3) to the answers (a–c). Write the letter.**

1 Whose act is the most dangerous? _____
2 Whose act is popular with people of all ages? _____
3 Whose act has the least movement? _____

a Juan Eze
b Marcel Debard
c Huang Jun

D **THINKING SKILL—Understand "Street entertainers are usually very talented." Do you agree or disagree? Give reasons.**

VOCABULARY

A **Match the bold words from the article in READING B to the definitions (1–8).**

1 _______________: doing something entertaining for an audience
2 _______________: a small model character that you move with your hands
3 _______________: an entertaining act that looks like magic
4 _______________: making something do what you want
5 _______________: moving in the air
6 _______________: not safe; likely to cause pain or harm
7 _______________: to push out air from your mouth
8 _______________: flames and heat from something burning

GRAMMAR indefinite pronouns

A Find and underline the indefinite pronouns in the article in READING B.

"Everywhere I go people always ask me what my trick is, but I never tell anyone the secret of my act. Nobody knows."

B Read the sentences and choose the correct option to complete the grammar rules.

Everywhere I go, people always ask me what my trick is.
We have to make sure nobody gets hurt.
Then, someone asked me to help.
I never tell anyone the secret of my act.
Everybody can see everything.

1. *Everywhere* means **all places / one or two places**.
2. *Nobody* means **some people / no people**.
3. *Someone* means **a specific person / an unknown person**.
4. If the verb or adverb is negative, use **anyone / someone**.
5. *Everything* means **all things / all people**.

For more practice, go to page 145.

C Read the paragraph and choose the correct option.

Before he became known to **1 someone / everyone / anyone** as James Bond, the actor Pierce Brosnan worked as a street entertainer in London. He was training to become an artist, but he met **2 somewhere / someone / something** who showed him the art of fire-eating. Soon after Brosnan started performing, **3 nobody / everybody / somebody** who worked as a circus agent saw his act and thought it was amazing. Brosnan performed his fire-eating trick on the TV show *Muppets Tonight*. **4 Nobody / Everyone / Everything** knows exactly how it happened, but there was a problem with the fire-eating trick and Pierce got serious burns. In true James Bond style, he didn't let **5 anyone / everybody / nobody** know he was hurt until the end of the show.

D IN PAIRS How popular are the types of entertainment in the box? Discuss. Use indefinite pronouns.

going to a music concert	going to a sports event	playing board games	watching TV
going to a play	going to the movies	playing video games	

A: I know someone who likes …
A: Nobody spends much time …
B: I think everyone likes …
B: I don't know anyone who likes …

SPEAKING

A Think about the street entertainers that you see in your country. Make notes about:

- where you usually see them
- what they do
- how you feel about them
- how you think others feel about them

B IN PAIRS Discuss street entertainers. Try to talk for at least one minute. Use the Confident Communicator box to help you.

I usually see entertainers in the main square. One guy plays the guitar …

CONFIDENT COMMUNICATOR
START TALKING

When you need to talk for a minute or more, try to make notes about what you want to say before you start talking. You can look at your notes as you speak to help you remember what you want to say.

The Music Industry

LISTENING

A **Where can you find good music videos? How often do you watch them? Discuss as a class.**

B **3.02 LISTENING SKILL—Listen for numbers Listen to this interview with a music producer. Then complete the statements.**

1 Michael Jackson's music video for *Thriller* was ____________ minutes long.
2 *Gangnam Style*, a music video from Korea, became popular in ____________.
3 In 2017, the music video for the song *Despacito* had ____________ billion views on YouTube.

C **3.02 Listen again. Choose *True* or *False*.**

1 Scott Fleming used to be in a band. True / False
2 He used to be a DJ. True / False
3 Scott Fleming writes songs for bands. True / False
4 Most bands still write their own music. True / False
5 Music videos started an important change in the music industry. True / False
6 Today, anyone can make a music video and post it to YouTube. True / False

D **THINKING SKILL—Evaluate Can a good music video make a song popular? Give examples.**

VOCABULARY the music industry

A **Match the job descriptions (1–8) to the jobs (a–h). Write the letter.**

This person …

1 writes songs for a band. _____	a producer
2 is the main singer in a band. _____	b lead vocalist
3 controls the band's business side. _____	c songwriter
4 makes music videos. _____	d backup singer
5 sings in the background. _____	e stylist
6 records the songs in a music studio. _____	f sound technician
7 checks equipment so the audience can hear the band. _____	g manager
8 focuses on the band's clothes, hair, and makeup. _____	h director

B **IN PAIRS Imagine you could have one of the jobs from A. Which one would you like to have and why? Discuss.**

A: I would like to be a backup singer. You get to sing with different bands.

B: Yeah, that sounds like fun. I like fashion, so I think I'd like to be a stylist.

GRAMMAR used to

A **Read sentences from the interview. Then choose the correct option.**

Bands **used to** write their own music.
People **used to** listen to music on the radio.
Did you **use to** be in a band?
People **didn't use to** do that.

1 *Used to* is used for a past action that **is still happening now** / **isn't happening now**.
2 After *used to*, use the **–*ing*** / **base** form of the verb.
3 In questions and negative statements, use ***used to*** / ***use to***.

For more practice, go to page 145.

B Complete the sentences with *used to*, *didn't use to*, or *did* … *use to*.

1 Where ____________ you ____________ take music lessons?
2 I ____________ download music, but now I download music every week.
3 ____________ Tom ____________ work in a music store?
4 Those guys ____________ be in a band called Kings and Queens.
5 That restaurant ____________ be a movie theater.
6 My brother ____________ like hip hop, but he does now.
7 ____________ you ____________ watch cartoons when you were a kid?
8 Where ____________ they ____________ live?

C IN PAIRS Make questions with *Did* … *use to*. Use the phrases below and your own ideas. Then ask and answer the questions.

- watch music videos on TV
- wear a school uniform
- take music lessons
- hang out with friends at the mall

A: Did you use to watch music videos on TV? *B: Yes, I did. / No, I didn't.*

MAKE IT REAL

You can also use *would* to talk about something that happened in the past.
When I was younger, I used to watch music videos all the time.
When I was younger, I would watch music videos all the time.
Don't use *would* to describe a past state.
I used to live in Mexico City.
~~*I would live in Mexico City.*~~

PRONUNCIATION reduced form of *used to*

A 3.03 Listen to the sentences. Notice how the speakers reduce *used to* as /justə/.

B IN PAIRS Practice saying the questions and answers. Use the reduced form of *used to*.

1 A: Did you use to work in marketing? B: No, I used to work in information technology.
2 A: Did you use to walk to the office? B: No, I used to take the bus.
3 A: Did your parents use to own a restaurant? B: No, they used to own a bakery.

SPEAKING

A How did your parents or grandparents do these activities when they were your age? How do you do them now? Make notes in your notebook.

- watch movies
- contact family or friends
- do math problems
- listen to music
- take pictures

B IN GROUPS Compare your ideas. Use the Confident Communicator box to help you.

A: I think my parents used to listen to CDs when they were my age. I listen to music online.
B: My parents used to watch DVDs. I stream movies online.

CONFIDENT COMMUNICATOR
START TALKING

To ask another person his or her opinion or experience about the same topic, use one of these questions:
And you?
What about you?
How about you?

LESSON 3 Viewing Habits

VOCABULARY TV viewing

A Complete the definitions (1–7) with words from the box.

binge-watch channel-surf commercials episode on demand stream TV series

1 ______________ (*adjective*): ready to watch at any time
2 ______________ (*verb*): to go quickly from one channel to another looking for something to watch
3 ______________ (*noun plural*): a set of TV shows with the same characters
4 ______________ (*noun*): a TV program that is one part of a set
5 ______________ (*verb*): to play a video or game using wi-fi without downloading it
6 ______________ (*verb*): to watch several shows in a TV series at one time
7 ______________ (*noun*): advertisements on TV

B Complete the text with words from A.

1 This show is not ______________. You can only watch it on Saturday at 6 p.m.
2 When I don't know what to watch on TV, I ______________ until I find something I like.
3 My favorite TV ______________ is at 8 p.m. every Tuesday night.
4 Did you watch last night's ______________ of *City Hospital*? It was amazing!
5 On rainy evenings, I like to stay home and ______________ my favorite show.
6 There is no wi-fi here, so I can't ______________ that video on my computer.
7 When I watch TV, I often get a snack during the ______________.

C IN PAIRS Think about the TV shows you like and don't like. Say why you like them and how you watch them.

A: I like funny TV series. Sometimes I binge-watch … *B: I stream episodes of a TV series called …*

LISTENING

A Look at the pictures. Which one is most similar to the way you watch TV?

a

b

c

d

B 3.04 LISTENING SKILL—Identify opinions Listen to four people talk about their TV viewing habits. Match each speaker to a picture in A.

1 Speaker 1: ______ 2 Speaker 2: ______ 3 Speaker 3: ______ 4 Speaker 4: ______

C 3.04 **Listen again. Write the speaker who expresses each opinion.**

This person…

1. thinks there wasn't so much choice in the past. Speaker ______
2. says he/she doesn't watch very much TV. Speaker ______
3. likes watching foreign-language TV shows. Speaker ______
4. watches TV shows at the same time as doing something else. Speaker ______
5. isn't interested in watching TV commercials. Speaker ______
6. likes watching things that make him/her laugh. Speaker ______

MAKE IT REAL

To talk about something you like or enjoy doing, use the phrase *to be into.*

I'm really into police dramas. I love them!

D **THINKING SKILL—Evaluate** **How much time do you usually spend watching TV in a day? How does your amount compare to your classmates?**

WRITING

A **Read the text. Underline the three words the writer uses to make contrasts.**

I used to watch TV with my brother, but now that I'm older, I stream videos and TV series on my laptop. I rarely watch TV these days, although there are some shows I like. I still watch them, though I don't usually watch them on TV. I watch them online. The only time I watch TV is when I watch soccer on the weekend with my friends.

B **Make notes comparing your viewing habits in the past and your viewing habits now.**

In the past	Now
shows I watched:	shows I watch:
how I watched them:	how I watch them:
who I watched them with:	who I watch them with:

C **In your notebook, write a paragraph comparing your viewing habits now with your viewing habits in the past. Use *but*, *although*, and *though* to make contrasts.**

I used to ... but now ...

D **IN PAIRS** **Share your paragraphs from C. Suggest other ways to make contrasts between the past and now.**

SPEAKING

A **Check (✓) all the activities that you like to do.**

- ☐ watch TV with my friends and family
- ☐ watch TV alone
- ☐ stream shows on my computer, laptop, or phone
- ☐ watch TV while I'm doing something else
- ☐ watch shows I download on my computer, laptop, or phone
- ☐ watch TV in bed
- ☐ watch only one or two YouTube channels or TV series

B **IN GROUPS** **Ask and answer questions about viewing habits. Use the Confident Communicator box to help you.**

A: Do you like to watch TV? B: Yes, sometimes. I like watching …

CONFIDENT COMMUNICATOR

KEEP TALKING

Use the following qualifying phrases with adjectives to make what you're saying more interesting:

sort of / kind of *really/pretty*

My favorite show is a science fiction series. It's kind of / sort of scary and funny.

Did you see the new episode? It was pretty/really good.

Language and Life

Decision-making – Saving a Theater

A **Do you go to the movie theater? If so, which movie theaters do you go to? Do they look like any of the theaters in the article in B?**

B **3.05 Read the article about movie theaters. Then complete the sentences.**

LET'S GO TO THE MOVIES!

Nowadays, large movie theaters (called multiplexes) are everywhere. They have many screens showing different movies. They show 2D and 3D movies. Some show IMAX movies on giant-sized screens. Some also stream live theater shows or music concerts. In addition, some movie theaters that used to sell only popcorn and candy now have restaurants or cafés where you can enjoy a meal before or after the show. Because of competition from TV movies and home entertainment, movie theaters must find new ways to get people back into their seats. Some movie theaters now provide an experience where the audience dresses in costumes or sings along to the music. Outdoor or rooftop movie theaters are popular in some cities in the summer. You can also go to a drive-in movie theater (where you watch the movie in your car). There are about 400 drive-in movie theaters in the US today, although they're not as popular as in the 1950s and '60s.

In the past, almost everyone went to the movies. No one had a TV, so it was an exciting form of entertainment. Many beautiful movie theaters opened in the 1920s and '30s when people of all ages went to see the latest Hollywood movie on the big screen. Some of these theaters, such as the Pathé Tuschinski movie theater in Amsterdam and the Orinda Theater in California, are still open today. However, many of the old buildings that used to be movie theaters now have other uses or are closed.

1 Another word for a large movie theater is ____________.
2 At an IMAX movie, the screen is ____________.
3 In the summer, ____________, ____________, and ____________ theaters are popular.
4 In the US, drive-in movies were popular in the ____________ and ____________.

C **IN PAIRS** Read the ad from a local newspaper. Then make notes about your answers to the questions.

DO YOU LOVE WATCHING MOVIES?

Are you between the ages of 16 and 25? Then we'd love to hear from you!

We are looking for young people to help with ideas for our historic movie theater, The Ritzy. Opened in May 1922, it is a fine example of the magical days of Hollywood. Thanks to a large donation of $2 million, we can now make it ready for the 21st century! The Grand Re-opening is planned for the theater's 100th birthday in 2022.

To help with our project, contact us in writing with your answers to these questions:

- What kind of movies should we show?
- What foods and drinks should we sell?
- How much should tickets be?
- What other services should we provide?
- Should we have other events at the theater?
- What popular actors should we invite?
- What other ideas do you have for the Grand Re-opening?

We look forward to hearing from you!
The Ritzy Project Team

What movies to show?

______

______

Other services?

______

______

Eating options?

______

______

Other events at the theater?

______

______

Ticket prices?

______

______

Other ideas for the Grand Re-opening?

______

______

D **IN GROUPS** Share your ideas. Work together to write a clear, creative plan for the Grand Re-opening.

E Discuss the questions.

1 Were you able to make decisions with members of your group effectively? Why or why not?

2 In what other situations do you need to make decisions about a plan of action with others?

MAKE IT DIGITAL

Go online to find out about a historic movie theater that is popular today. How has it changed?

VOCABULARY review

SCORE: / 10

A Complete the sentences with the words from the box.

backup singer	blow	commercials	on demand	sound technician
binge-watch	channel-surf	dangerous	songwriter	stream

1 I usually ________ until I can find something I want to watch on TV.
2 I'm a ________ for the band. I check the equipment to make sure everything works right for the concert.
3 I like to watch ________. Some are funny, but they don't change my ideas about what to buy.
4 Be careful doing that trick. It's ________!
5 You can watch many shows anytime. Most of my favorite shows are available ________.
6 I don't really watch much TV, but I like to ________ music videos online.
7 One day I hope to be a famous singer, but right now I am a ________ for one.
8 I ________ my favorite shows on weekends. One Sunday afternoon, I watched eight episodes!
9 I'm not a good singer, but I'm good at creating words with music. I'm a good ________.
10 Did you see the street performer ________ fire from her mouth?

GRAMMAR review

SCORE: / 10

A Complete the sentences with the correct form of *used to*.

1 Did you ________ work at the music store downtown?
2 I didn't ________ like classical music, but I enjoy listening to it now.
3 Emile and Isaac ________ own a recording studio.
4 Did Paolo ________ be a street performer before he became an actor?
5 My grandmother ________ have a small black-and-white TV.

B Choose the correct option.

There was an amazing street entertainer that I saw every day on my way to work. **1** Everyone / Anyone watched him, but **2** no one / anyone understood how he did his trick. He looked like **3** nothing / something from a science fiction film because he wore a black and yellow robot costume. He used to stand very still until **4** something / someone walked past him. Then, he moved his body and changed shape until he looked like a small yellow truck. Then, he drove away. **5** Everybody / Somebody who saw his performance said it was amazing.

16–20 correct: You can discuss the music industry and TV viewing habits. You can use indefinite pronouns and the phrase *used to*.
0–15 correct: Look again at the Vocabulary and Grammar sections in the unit.

TOTAL SCORE: / 20

WHAT DO YOU KNOW NOW? Look back at page 27 and add words you know now to the boxes.

STUDY SKILLS DESIGNING A QUESTIONNAIRE

Take the quiz about questionnaires. Go to **Study Skills** on page 129 to find the answers. Then learn more about designing a questionnaire.

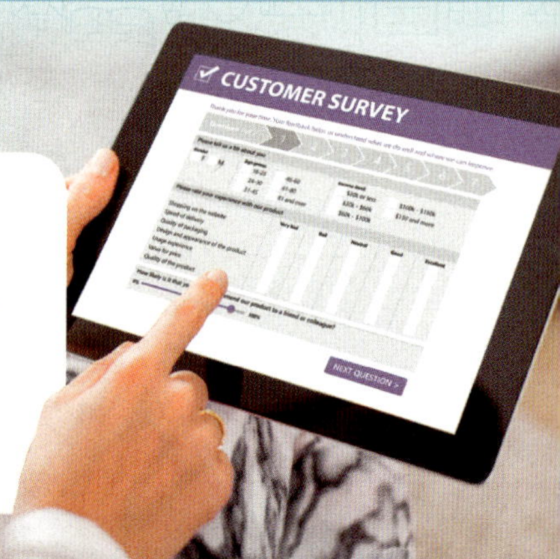

1 The language in a questionnaire should be as clear and simple as possible.
a True **b** False

2 What is the maximum number of questions your questionnaire should have?
a 5 **b** 10 **c** 20

3 On average, what percentage of people respond to surveys?
a 5% **b** 33% **c** 78%

UNIT

4 Your ID

WHAT DO YOU ALREADY KNOW?

1 Think of people you know. Write one word to describe each person.

2 IN PAIRS Share and compare your list. Say who the people are and describe them. Add more words to your list, if possible.

Person—Description

DISCUSS & SHARE

VIDEO

3 IN GROUPS Watch the video and answer the question.

SYM Are you an introvert or an extrovert?

In this unit, you will ...

- talk about personality types, describe people using superlatives, and compare appearance to others.
- use thinking skills: apply and predict.
- read about personality types in the workplace.
- use strategies to start and keep talking by showing disagreement, describing yourself in the past, and making comparisons.
- use interpersonal communication skills to understand and interact with different personalities.
- follow a school psychologist to learn about this job and the skills needed for a career in education.

READING

A **Think about your close friends. Are their personalities similar to or different from yours?**

B 4.01 **Read this article about different personality types. Then choose the correct option.**

WHAT'S YOUR PERSONALITY TYPE?

Are you friendly and outgoing? Or are you the quiet type? Do you like to work as part of a team or do you prefer to work alone? Psychologists try to understand people by studying their personalities. Read on to find out more about four different personality types.

Type As

Type As are often successful, professional people. They are very organized and focused, and they work hard to succeed. Sometimes, they can be **impatient** with co-workers who aren't as hard-working as they are. They enjoy taking risks, but get stressed easily.

Type Bs

Type Bs are usually **easygoing** and don't get stressed. They love to spend time with friends and have fun. Usually, they're cheerful and **optimistic**. Their worst characteristics are that they can be **lazy** and take a long time to make decisions.

Type Cs

Type Cs are interested in small details and numbers. They are very good problem solvers. They like to be alone and don't always like working as part of a team. They are often **shy** and find it hard to communicate. Type Cs get as stressed as Type As at work. Take time to relax, Type Cs!

Type Ds

Type Ds aren't as optimistic as Type Bs. In fact, they can be very pessimistic. They often worry, see the negative side of things, and get **depressed** when things are hard. They like to feel comfortable and don't like to take risks. However, they are patient and hard-working.

Remember that most people are a mix of these different types. It's unusual to find a person who is only one personality type.

1 Type D people **enjoy** / **don't enjoy** taking risks.
2 Type C people find it **easy** / **hard** to relax.
3 Type B people have a **positive** / **negative** view of the world.
4 Type A people **are** / **aren't** hard-working.

C **READING SKILL—Summarize** **Complete the summary for Type B people using words from the article in B.**

Type B people like having **1** ______________. They are usually sociable and **2** ______________. They have a/an **3** ______________ view of life, but they can be **4** ______________ and can take time to decide things.

D **THINKING SKILL—Apply** **Explain what personality type you think you are. Why? How about your friends and family?**

VOCABULARY

A **Match the words from the box to the definitions (1–6).**

depressed easygoing impatient lazy optimistic shy

1 ______________: quiet; nervous and embarrassed
2 ______________: very relaxed; calm
3 ______________: sad; very unhappy
4 ______________: not wanting to work
5 ______________: positive; thinking good things will happen
6 ______________: annoyed because something isn't happening quickly

GRAMMAR *(not) as … as*

A **Choose the sentence with the same meaning.**

1 Type Ds aren't as optimistic as Type Bs.
- **a** Types Ds and Type Bs are equally optimistic.
- **b** Type Ds are more optimistic than Type Bs.
- **c** Type Bs are more optimistic than Type Ds.

2 Type Cs are as stressed as Type As at work.
- **a** Type Cs and Type As are equally stressed at work.
- **b** Type Cs are more stressed than Type As at work.
- **c** Type As are more stressed than Type Cs at work.

For more practice, go to page 146.

B **Choose the correct option.**

Because my sister and I are twins, people think we have the same personality, but we are very different. My sister, Danni, is more of a Type A personality. I'm more of a Type B. Danni **1 isn't as patient as / is as patient as** I am. She gets mad about small things, but I don't. In general, Type A people **2 aren't as easygoing as / are as easygoing as** Type B people. Of course, Type B people aren't always relaxed. For example, I'm **3 as impatient as / not as impatient as** Danni when I have to wait in line at the store. We both want to buy our things and leave quickly! Danni and I are different, but we have a good relationship. I think we are both outgoing, and I'm **4 as friendly as / not as friendly as** her. For example, we both like going out together to see friends. But I'm **5 as hard-working as / not as hard-working as** Danni, so I go out more often! I usually stay out with friends longer, and she comes home and does her homework!

C IN PAIRS **Compare people. Use adjectives from the reading and any others you know.**

brother/sister   classmate/friend   Dad/Mom   Type A personalities/Type B personalities

My brother isn't as easygoing as my sister.

MAKE IT YOURS

Go online or use a dictionary to find more words for characteristics that you and your friends have.

PRONUNCIATION stress on the adjective

A 4.02 **Listen to the opinions. Notice the stress on the adjectives.**

B 4.03 IN PAIRS **Listen and repeat.**

1. I don't think swimming is as difficult as skiing.
2. I'm not as cheerful as my best friend.
3. Learning grammar isn't as easy as learning vocabulary.

SPEAKING

A IN PAIRS **Play a game of Guess Who. Think of a well known character from a movie or TV series. Describe their positive and negative characteristics. Ask your partner to guess who it is. Take turns.**

B IN GROUPS **Talk about what percent (%) of each personality type you think you are. Give reasons. Use the Confident Communicator box to help you.**

CONFIDENT COMMUNICATOR
KEEP TALKING

Use the following expressions to estimate:
I think I'm about/roughly/approximately 25% Type A, because …
Off the top of my head, I'd say I'm about 50% Type D, because …
I have a feeling I'm probably mostly a Type B, because …

Teamwork and Personality

VOCABULARY different personalities

A Match the types of people (1–6) to their descriptions (a–f). Write the letter.

1 A leader ____
2 An expert ____
3 A loner ____
4 A workaholic ____
5 A creative thinker ____
6 A risk taker ____

a likes to work a lot.
b likes to be alone.
c likes to try new and sometimes dangerous things.
d is responsible for a group of people.
e has specialized knowledge.
f has new and imaginative ideas.

B IN PAIRS Which type of person from A do you think you are? Which type(s) of people do you like to work with? Discuss and give reasons.

I think I am a creative thinker because I like to think of new ideas. I wouldn't like to work with a workaholic because …

LISTENING

A Do you prefer to work in a large group, in a small group, or alone? Discuss.

B 4.04 LISTENING SKILL—Identify tone Listen to the talk about teamwork and different personalities. What is the style of the talk? Choose and explain.

a serious b amusing c critical

C 4.04 Listen again. Choose *True* or *False*.

1 All the members of a team should have the same personality type. True / False
2 A good leader sometimes lets other members lead the team. True / False
3 Many companies have a technology expert on the team. True / False
4 Creative thinkers are often very organized. True / False
5 The information in the talk is only useful for people at work. True / False

D THINKING SKILL—Apply Think about groups/teams that you are in at school, at work, or in the community. Which role do you usually take? Which one do you prefer?

GRAMMAR superlative adjectives

A We use superlative adjectives to compare more than two things. Underline the superlatives.

1 An expert has the greatest knowledge about a subject important to the project.
2 The creative thinker is often not the most organized person on the team.
3 The expert will explain all the most important details to the team.
4 That is the worst mistake you can make!

B Choose the correct words to complete the rules.

1 Use *a* / *the* before a superlative adjective.
2 For adjectives that are one syllable, add *–er* / *–est* to the end of the word.
3 For adjectives that are two syllables and end with *–y*, add *–est* / *–iest* to the end of the word.
4 For adjectives that are two or more syllables, use *most* / *the most* before the adjective.
5 Some superlative forms are irregular: *bad–the worst; good–better* / *the best*.

For more practice, go to page 147.

C Complete the sentences with the correct superlative form of the adjective in parentheses.

1 Diana is ______________ (creative) person I know.
2 The day I won this award was ______________ (happy) day of my life.
3 Fernando is ______________ (tall) student in this class.
4 Esmeralda is ______________ (talkative) student in this class.
5 The Green Garden is ______________ (good) restaurant in town.

D IN PAIRS Discuss the questions.

1 What was the most exciting day of your life?
2 Who is the smartest person you know?
3 What is the most beautiful place you know of?
4 What is the worst thing to do on the weekend?
5 (Write your own question.)

____

____

MAKE IT REAL

In spoken English, people often use the superlative to show that something is really good or bad. In these cases, they often pronounce *the* /ðə/ as *thee* /ði/.

That was the /ði/ most amazing meal!

It was the /ði/ worst movie.

SPEAKING

A What were you like in your elementary school classes? Were you the funniest kid? The quietest kid? The smartest kid? The most creative kid?

B IN PAIRS Talk about how your personality changed as you grew up. Are you different now?

When I was in kindergarten, I was the most creative kid in the class. But in first grade …

C IN GROUPS Say how your partner's personality changed as he or she grew up. Did anything surprise you? Use the Confident Communicator box to help you.

CONFIDENT COMMUNICATOR
KEEP TALKING

Use these phrases to talk about changes in your life:
When I was younger / in kindergarten / in high school, I was talkative.
I used to be a little impatient, but I'm more relaxed now.
Until I went to high school / university, I was the shiest person in the class.

Who Are You Like?

VOCABULARY characteristics

A Complete the sentences with words from the box.

adventurous bossy generous honest rude selfish smart

Someone who is …

1 ______________ tells people what to do.
2 ______________ is intelligent.
3 ______________ isn't polite.
4 ______________ enjoys giving things to people.
5 ______________ loves new and exciting experiences.
6 ______________ thinks only about himself or herself.
7 ______________ tells the truth.

B Complete the table with the words in A.

Positive characteristics	Negative characteristics

C IN PAIRS Compare your answers from B. Can you add any other characteristics?

D IN GROUPS Choose one characteristic from A that describes you and one that does not. Explain.

I think I'm very generous. I love giving gifts. So, I don't think I'm selfish.

LISTENING

A Look at the pictures. Guess how the people are related. Use the words from the box to help you.

A: I think these two are father and son. He's the oldest because …

B: I don't think they're father and son. I think they're …

aunt/niece brother/sister brothers cousins father/daughter father/son mother/daughter mother/son sisters twins

______________ ______________ ______________ ______________

B 4.05 Listen to the speakers talk about who they are like. Then match each speaker to his or her picture in A.

1 Speaker 1: photo _____
2 Speaker 2: photo _____
3 Speaker 3: photo _____
4 Speaker 4: photo _____

C 4.05 **LISTENING SKILL—Listen for detail** **Listen again and choose the words the speakers use to describe themselves.**

Speaker 1: tall / bossy / creative / blond hair / blue eyes
Speaker 2: short / tall / slim / brown hair / blond / adventurous / smart
Speaker 3: brown eyes / small / selfish / brown hair
Speaker 4: bald / tall / easygoing / strict

D **THINKING SKILL—Predict** **As people grow older, do they become more similar to their parents and grandparents in appearance? How about in personality?**

WRITING

A **Read the description of a character from a movie. Can you guess who the character is?**

One of my favorite characters is ▇▇▇ from the movie ▇▇▇. The American actor Harrison Ford plays this role. He is a pilot and the leader of the Rebel Alliance. In the early movies, he travels around the galaxy with his copilot, Chewbacca. He's easygoing and very smart, but he is sometimes rude. Princess Leia is in love with him, but she says she is not. They get married in the end and have a son named Ben. I really like him because he's a hero, but he's not perfect.

B **You are going to write a description of a character from a movie, TV show, or book. Make notes about ...**

the movie, TV show, or book __________
the character's appearance __________
the character's personality __________
what the character does __________
how you feel about the character __________

C **Write your description in your notebook. Try to write about 100 words.**

SPEAKING

A **IN PAIRS** **Compare yourself to a member of your family. Describe how you are the same or different. Use the Confident Communicator box to help you. Consider the criteria.**

- physical appearance, e.g. hair color, eye color, hair type (e.g. wavy, straight, curly), weight, height
- your personality
- interests and abilities, e.g. artistic ability, sports, music, career

I'm like my dad. We are both adventurous. But I look like my mom and my aunt.

CONFIDENT COMMUNICATOR
KEEP TALKING

Use the following phrases to talk about who you are like:
I look like/don't look like my mom/dad.
I take after/don't take after my mom/dad.

Use the following phrases to talk about characteristics:
I'm like/not like my mom/dad.
My brother/sister and I are alike/not alike.

Language and Life

Interpersonal Communication – Working with Different Personalities

A 4.06 **Read the conversation. Decide which person has each type of personality.**

Lana: Thanks for coming to the meeting. I made notes on the things we need to do. I think we need to focus on this year's fundraiser and organize it.

Ben: A fundraiser? We tried that last year. You know, we spent a lot of money on T-shirts, and we didn't make any money. I think that's a bad idea.

Lana: How much money did we make? And how much did we lose? Alex?

Alex: I have that information right here. We spent $456 on T-shirts, and we made $153. We had a lot of T-shirts that didn't sell. We also spent $120 on food and drink.

Marta: I think fundraisers are fun! I had a great time at the one last year and I think people enjoyed it. OK, so we didn't sell many T-shirts, but maybe we can do something different this year, like have a raffle or a popcorn stand.

Ben: A popcorn stand? I hate popcorn.

Marta: OK, maybe not popcorn. How about we sell cookies? Everyone loves cookies! I can make some.

Alex: Maybe we should find out how much the ingredients cost and how many we need to make. I'm happy to do that.

Lana: Those are all interesting ideas, but I think we need to focus on two things. First, we need to decide on a date for the fundraiser and second, which person can do which job. I think that would be very useful. Alex, take notes, please …

1 Type A ____________ **2** Type B ____________ **3** Type C ____________ **4** Type D ____________

B **Choose the adjective that describes each person.**

1	Lana:	organized	easygoing	lazy
2	Ben:	focused	negative	relaxed
3	Alex:	selfish	bossy	logical
4	Marta:	cheerful	pessimistic	honest

C Read lines from the rest of the conversation. Who do you think said each line?

Alex Ben Lana Marta

1 ______________: "I think we should forget about a fundraiser. I don't think people will come."

2 ______________: "These are great ideas. Having a popcorn stand, having a raffle, selling cookies ... I'm sure we can make money!"

3 ______________: "We really need to make a decision by the end of this meeting. We can't wait another week. We have to get started as soon as possible!"

4 ______________: "It's good to know how much money we can make. Popcorn is cheap to make, but we can sell it for a lot more money, I think."

D IN GROUPS Prepare a role-play about planning a class event, such as a party or a celebration. Use the suggested phrases to help you.

Student A: You have a Type A personality.
Suggested phrases:
I made notes on ...
I think we need to focus on ...
First, we should decide ...

Student B: You have a Type B personality.
Suggested phrases:
... is / are fun!
I love ...!
These are great ideas!

Student C: You have a Type C personality.
Suggested phrases:
I have that information ...
Maybe we should find out how much ...
I am happy to ...

Student D: You have a Type D personality.
Suggested phrases:
We tried that ...
I think that's a bad idea...
I don't think people ...

E Role-play your discussion from D for the class. Can your classmates guess who played each personality type?

F Discuss the questions.

1 Did you understand the different personalities better in the role play? Why or why not?

2 In what other situations do you need to interact successfully with people who have different personalities?

MAKE IT DIGITAL

Go online to find a quiz about personality types. Take the quiz and share your results with the class.

VOCABULARY review

SCORE: / 10

A Match the personality types (1–5) to their synonyms (a–e). Write the letter.

1 easygoing ____	**a** happy
2 depressed ____	**b** worried
3 outgoing ____	**c** friendly
4 stressed ____	**d** relaxed
5 cheerful ____	**e** unhappy

B Complete the sentences with words from the box.

expert leader loner risk taker workaholic

1 My best friend is a real ____________. He isn't afraid of anything and loves anything dangerous!
2 I was a ____________ when I was teenager. I didn't want to make friends with anyone.
3 My eldest daughter is a ____________. She works very long hours.
4 Dr. Milagros is a psychology ____________. She knows a lot about how people think and behave.
5 John is the ____________ of this project. He tells everyone else on the team what to do.

GRAMMAR review

SCORE: / 10

A Complete the sentences using *as ... as* and the adjectives in parentheses.

1 Jack ______________________________ as Garth. (not/tall)
2 Emily ______________________________ Marty. (shy)
3 Greg and Henry ______________________________ Barbara. (not/outgoing)
4 Uncle Garth ______________________________ Dad. (cheerful)
5 Raul and his sister ______________________________ Patty. (not/hard-working)

B Complete the sentences using the superlative form of the adjectives in parentheses.

1 My brother is ______________________________ (smart) person in our family.
2 Auntie Jill is ______________________________ (creative) person I know.
3 That was ______________________________ (scary) movie ever! I didn't like it.
4 Martina is ______________________________ (best) manager in the office.
5 Fernando is ______________________________ (young) child in the Perez family.

16–20 correct: You can identify different personalities and characteristics. You can use superlative adjectives.
0–15 correct: Look again at the Vocabulary and Grammar sections in the unit.

TOTAL SCORE: / 20

WHAT DO YOU KNOW NOW? Look back at page 37 and add words you know now to the box.

FOLLOW A PRO EDUCATION

Take the quiz about education. Then go to Follow A Pro on page 130. Find the answers and learn more about education.

1 How many students does the largest school in the world, in India, have?
a 15,000 **b** 25,000 **c** 55,000

2 How much time do elementary school students in China spend on homework each day?
a about one hour **b** about two hours **c** about three hours

3 What is the oldest English-speaking university in the world?
a Oxford **b** Cambridge **c** Yale

UNIT 5 Prepping

WHAT DO YOU ALREADY KNOW?

1 Think about the types of plans or arrangements you often make. Write the words.

2 IN PAIRS Share and compare your information. Add more words to your list.

Events

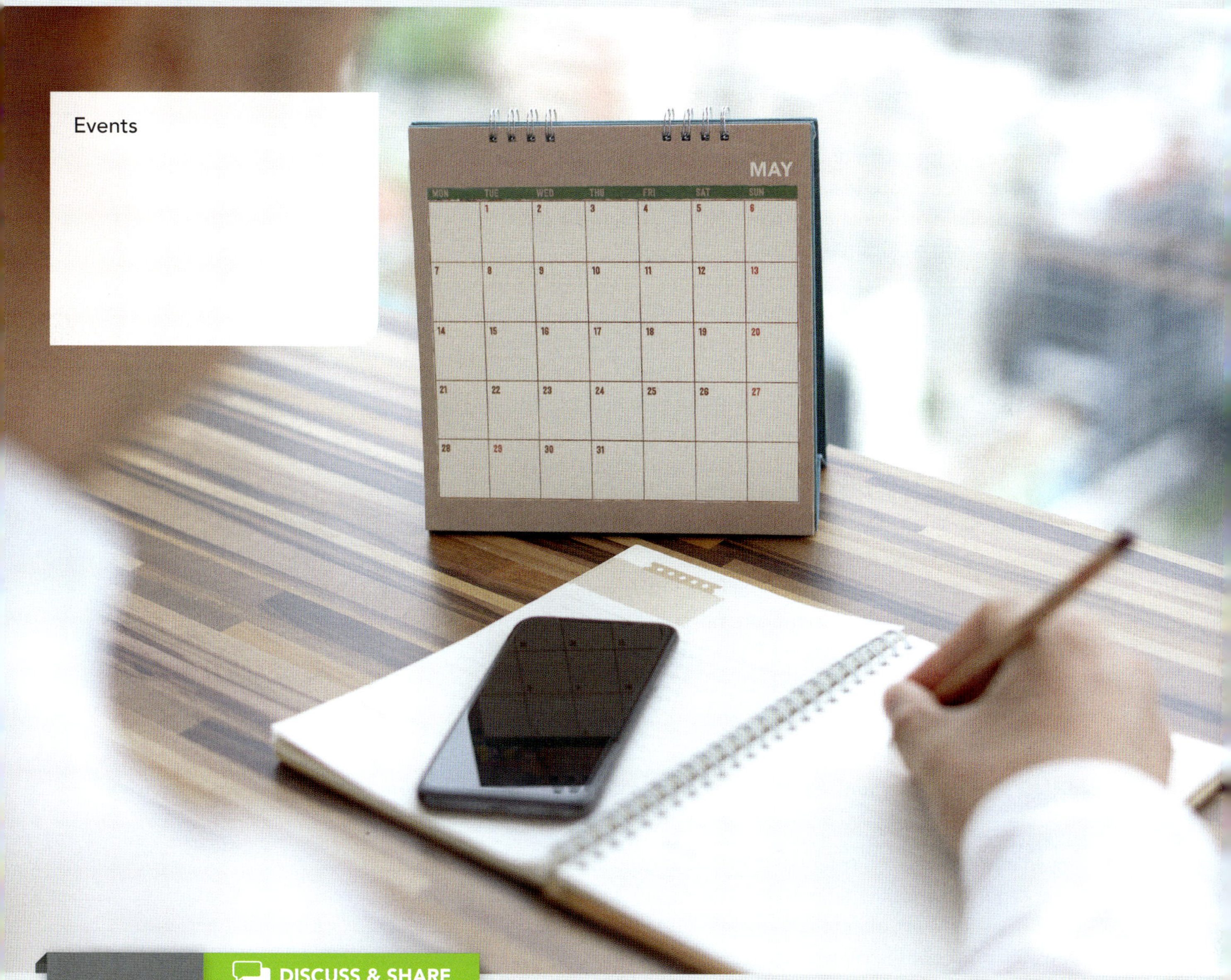

DISCUSS & SHARE

VIDEO

3 IN GROUPS Watch the video and answer the question.

SYM Do you do one thing at a time, or are you a multi-tasker?

In this unit, you will ...

- talk about making arrangements for a hotel, a school event, and a wedding.
- use thinking skills: predict, remember, and analyze.
- read a dialogue about checking a hotel reservation.
- use strategies to keep talking by making requests and practicing before giving a talk.
- use global competence skills to understand and appreciate social customs.
- learn research skills for school and work.

Thanks for Your Help

READING

A THINKING SKILL—Predict Look at the pictures in B and read the first line of the conversation. Predict the answers.

1 What do you think the customer's first question to the clerk will be?
2 How do you think the clerk will answer?

B 5.01 Read the conversation between the hotel clerk and the customer. Why is Shiro calling the hotel?

Clerk: Bonjour, Hôtel Paris.
Shiro: Hello. Uh … Do you speak English?
Clerk: Of course, sir. Good morning. How can I help you?
Shiro: Good morning. My name is Shiro Ito. My wife and I have a **reservation** for four nights starting tomorrow, but we have a problem. Your website says that check-in time is two o'clock, but our **flight** arrives at eight a.m. We'd like to **check in** at about eleven o'clock if possible.
Clerk: We probably won't have rooms before two, but I'll check to see if any rooms might be ready early. One moment, sir … I'm sorry, Mr. Ito, but I can't check you in at eleven. However, I can check you in at 1:30, and I can give you a **voucher** for a free lunch in our restaurant. They have a very nice **buffet**.
Shiro: That's fine, thank you. We'll eat lunch while we wait.
Clerk: Good. We'll take care of your **luggage** at the front desk while you have lunch. I think you'll like our restaurant. The food is excellent, and you won't feel so tired if you have some of our good French coffee!
Shiro: I'm sure we'll enjoy the meal, but I won't have coffee because I want to sleep in the afternoon.
Clerk: I understand, sir. Have a good flight, and we'll see you tomorrow.
Shiro: Thanks for your help.
Clerk: You're welcome, Mr. Ito.

C READING SKILL—Scan Look back at the conversation to find the answers to the questions as quickly as possible.

1 How many nights is the reservation for? ______
2 What is normal check-in time at the hotel? ______
3 What does the clerk offer to give them? ______
4 Does Shiro accept the offer? ______
5 Why doesn't he want to have coffee? ______

VOCABULARY

A Match the words (1–6) to their definitions (a–f). Write the letter.

1 reservation ____
2 check in ____
3 flight ____
4 voucher ____
5 buffet ____
6 luggage ____

a a lot of food on a table for people to choose
b a trip on an airplane
c an arrangement for something to be kept for you to use later
d bags and suitcases that you take on a trip
e to register at a hotel or for a flight
f a piece of paper that you can use in place of money

GRAMMAR modals of intention, offer, and prediction

A Read the sentences from the conversation in READING B. Label the sentences *P* (prediction), *I* (intention), or *O* (offer).

1 I'll check to see if any rooms might be ready early. ____
2 We probably won't have rooms before two. ____
3 I can check you in at 1:30, and I can give you a voucher for a free lunch in our restaurant. ____
4 We'll eat lunch while we wait. ____
5 I think you'll like our restaurant. ____
6 I won't have coffee because I want to sleep in the afternoon. ____

For more practice, go to page 148.

B Complete the sentences with *will*, *won't*, or *can*.

1 We ____________ probably check out before eleven.
2 I think the weather ____________ be nice tomorrow.
3 I ____________ help you with your reservation if you want.
4 I ____________ have a big lunch because I don't want to feel sleepy.
5 I don't think you ____________ like that restaurant. The food isn't very good.

C Read the conversations and write an appropriate intention, offer, or prediction.

1 A: I can't read the menu because I don't understand French.
B: (offer) ____________________
2 A: What are you going to order?
B: (intention) ____________________
3 A: This hotel's restaurant has very good reviews.
B: (prediction) Yes. ____________________

D IN PAIRS Compare your sentences from C and discuss. Did you have similar ideas? Then practice your conversations together.

SPEAKING

A IN PAIRS Practice a conversation between a hotel receptionist and a guest who is checking in. Read the instructions for each role. Use the Confident Communicator box to help you.

Receptionist: Explain that you have a room on the ground floor near the pool or a room on the 12th floor. Predict why the guest might like each room.
Guest: Tell the receptionist which room you will take and what you intend to do during your stay.

B Role play your conversation for the class or for another pair.

CONFIDENT COMMUNICATOR
KEEP TALKING

Use the following expressions to express intentions and predictions.

Predictions:
*I **think** you'll like the restaurant. / You'll **probably** like the restaurant. / **I'm sure** you'll like the restaurant*

Intentions:
*I **think** I'll have fish. / I'll **probably** have fish. / I **guess** I'll have fish.*

LESSON 2 Party On!

LISTENING

A Discuss the questions about parties as a class.

1 Why do you and your friends usually have parties?
2 How often do you go to parties?

B 5.02 **LISTENING SKILL—Listen for gist** **Listen to two conversations. Then answer the questions.**

1 What are the two conversations about? ______
2 What are the students celebrating? ______
3 What do they need permission for? ______
4 Does Ms. Jenkins give them permission? ______
5 Which conversation is more formal? Why? ______

C 5.02 **THINKING SKILL—Remember** **List the party preparations the students talked about in the first conversation. Listen again to check your list.**

1 *the date*
2 ______
3 ______
4 ______
5 ______

VOCABULARY making suggestions

A Complete the conversation with the phrases from the box.

a suggestion	let ... know	What about
How about	Let's	Why don't

Jen: OK, **1** ______ talk about the party. Where can we have it?
Yao: **2** ______ we have it at Paul's house? He has a swimming pool.
Jen: Awesome! **3** ______ food and drinks?
Ana: Tony and I can bring food. Could you guys bring the drinks?
Yao: Can I make **4** ______?
Ana: Sure.
Yao: **5** ______ asking everyone to bring one thing to eat and one thing to drink?
Jen: Good idea. I'll talk to Paul and **6** ______ you ______ about having the party at his house.
Ana: Cool. Text us, OK?
Jen: I will.

B IN PAIRS Use the cues to write short conversations. Then practice the conversations with your partner.

1 A: How about ______ after class tomorrow?
B: I don't know. How about ______?
A: Maybe. I'll ______ and let you know.
B: OK, no problem.

2 A: How about ______ on Saturday?
B: OK, why don't we ______?
A: Can I ______?
B: Sure.
A: What about ______?
B: Cool.

GRAMMAR modals of request and permission

A 5.02 **Listen to the conversations and complete the examples with *can*, *can't*, *could*, and *may*. Listen again to check your answers.**

1 ____________ you talk to the director about that? (formal request)
2 ____________ you design an invitation? (informal request)
3 ____________ I talk to you for a minute? (formal permission)
4 ____________ we use the auditorium for it? (formal permission)
5 ____________ I make a suggestion? (informal permission)
6 You ____________ stay after 10 p.m. (refusal of permission)

For more practice, go to page 148.

B Number the sentences from the conversation in order.

__1__ Zara: Great news, guys! Ms. Jenkins says we can use the auditorium.
____ Lucas: Yes, 10 o'clock is fine. What else do we need to plan?
____ Mika: We need decorations. Lucas, can you design some posters to put on the walls?
____ Zara: Yes, it's fantastic. We can't stay after 10 p.m., but that's OK, I think.
____ Mika: Zara and I will write the text. Mr. Wilson, could you check our English?
____ Lucas: Sure. I can do the design, but my English isn't great, so I can't write the text.
____ Mr. Wilson: Of course. OK, we have to go to class now.
____ Lucas: That's awesome news!

C IN GROUPS Read the conversation in B aloud to check your answers.

D IN PAIRS Find one example each of an offer, permission, a formal request, an informal request, and a refusal of permission in B.

PRONUNCIATION word stress with modal auxiliaries

A 5.03 **Listen to the sentences. Underline the modal auxiliary if it is stressed. Then practice reading the sentences aloud using the correct word stress.**

1 I can make a cake.
2 May I invite my boyfriend?
3 Could you help me, please?
4 I can design an invitation.
5 I won't have coffee.
6 We can't invite friends.

SPEAKING

A IN GROUPS Plan a class party. Ask questions and make suggestions and offers. Make notes about your decisions in your notebook.

B Describe your plan to your class. You can refer to your notes and the Confident Communicator box to help you. Vote on the best party plan.

A: We can have our party at …, but we can't …

B: Paula says she'll bring … She's also going to …

CONFIDENT COMMUNICATOR
KEEP TALKING

Remember to use formal or informal language, depending on the situation.
Requests
Formal: *Could you …? Yes, of course. / Certainly.*
Informal: *Can you …? Sure. / No problem.*

Permission
Formal: *May I …? / Could I …? Yes, you may. / Of course. / Certainly.*
Informal: *Can I …? Go ahead. / Sure. / Yeah, no problem.*

LISTENING

A Look at the picture and answer the questions in your notebook.

1 How is this wedding similar to weddings in your country?
2 How is it different?

B 5.04 LISTENING SKILL—Listen for main ideas Listen to two friends talking. Then answer the questions.

1 What is the topic of the conversation?

____

2 Are Susana and Jessica both invited to the event?

____

C 5.04 Listen again. Then choose the correct answer.

1 Susana is **excited** / **nervous** about going to the wedding.
2 This wedding is in a **church** / **outside**.
3 The wedding **is** / **is not** very formal.
4 Jessica tells Susana to buy a wedding gift **in a store** / **online**.
5 The wedding and the reception are **in the same place** / **in different places**.
6 Jessica offers to **take Susana to the wedding** / **give Susana directions to the wedding**.

D THINKING SKILL—Analyze In your opinion, why does Susana have a lot of questions about the wedding?

VOCABULARY wedding customs

A Match the words and phrases from the box to the definitions (1–8).

accept an invitation	gift registry	send an RSVP	wedding
dress up	pick up	show up	wedding reception

1 ____________________: a ceremony for two people to get married
2 ____________________: to agree to attend an event or social activity
3 ____________________: a formal party after a wedding ceremony
4 ____________________: a list of things online or in a store that a person or a couple would like to receive
5 ____________________: to wear clothes that are more formal than usual
6 ____________________: to arrive in a place or at an event
7 ____________________: to take a person somewhere in a vehicle
8 ____________________: to let someone know if you are going to attend an event

B IN PAIRS Discuss the questions about weddings in your country.

1 Where do people usually have weddings?
2 Is there usually a reception after the wedding? If so, what happens at the reception?
3 Do couples have gift registries online or at stores? What are some typical wedding gifts?

MAKE IT YOURS

Make a list of words that describe wedding customs in your country.

WRITING

A Read a short essay about American weddings. Then answer the questions.

American Wedding Customs

In the US, some people have very traditional wedding ceremonies, but others prefer nontraditional ceremonies. Many people get married in places like event centers or even at home. Some weddings are in the morning, but most weddings are in the afternoon or the evening. If you receive a wedding invitation, you should send an RSVP. You can do this online if the wedding couple has a wedding website. There is usually an online gift registry so that you can send gifts directly to the bride and groom. Guests at traditional weddings usually wear suits and dresses. People also dress up for nontraditional weddings, but the clothes are usually a little less formal.

On the day of the wedding, the bride and groom do not see each other before the ceremony. In traditional weddings, the bride walks to the groom with her father, but now some brides walk with both parents. After the ceremony, there is a wedding reception, where there's a big meal, and friends and family members give short speeches. There is usually a band or a DJ, and people dance and celebrate through the night with the newly married couple.

1 Where do people get married? ____________________
2 At what time of day do people get married? ____________________
3 Where do people usually buy wedding gifts? ____________________
4 What do guests wear to weddings? ____________________
5 What happens at the wedding? ____________________
6 What happens after the wedding ceremony? ____________________

B Use the questions in A to make notes about typical weddings in your country. Add other information if you want to.

C Use your notes from B to write in your notebook about weddings in your country.

D IN PAIRS Read each other's texts from C. Are your descriptions similar? Compare and discuss.

SPEAKING

A Make notes about another social event you attended.

Type of event ____________________
Location and time ____________________
Clothing ____________________
Ceremony ____________________
Other activities ____________________
Other information ____________________

B IN GROUPS Tell your group about the social event from A. Use the Confident Communicator box to help you.

CONFIDENT COMMUNICATOR
START TALKING

Before you give a talk, practice it. Remember that you can refer to your notes while you are talking to help you remember what to say, but you need to look at your audience, so it's a good idea to practice your talk several times.

Language and Life

Global Competence – Give Advice about Social Customs

A 5.05 **Read the excerpt from a guidebook to the US. Then choose *True* or *False*.**

Social Customs in the US

When you travel to another country, it is important to understand the customs of the country. Here are some useful tips for visitors to the US.

GREETINGS

- When Americans meet someone for the first time, especially in business situations, they usually shake hands. Young people do not usually shake hands in informal situations. Kissing on the cheek is not a common form of greeting.
- At small social events, Americans sometimes greet each person, but normally people say hello to the group in general.
- Use a person's title (Mr., Ms., Dr.) and last name in business situations or when the other person is much older than you. Never use a title with a first name.

SOCIAL EVENTS

- Do not accept an invitation to an event if you don't plan to go. Simply say something like, "I'm sorry, but I have plans that evening. Thanks for the invitation."
- For a dinner party, arrive on time or no more than 5 or 10 minutes late. For an informal party, you can arrive and leave at any time.
- It is typical to take a small gift like flowers or chocolate to a dinner party but not to more informal events.

FOOD AND RESTAURANTS

- In restaurants, Americans often divide the bill so that everyone pays an equal part. If someone says, "My treat," or "I'll get it," that person will pay the bill. Don't argue. Just thank the person.
- If you invite someone to go out to eat, ask if there are foods that they can't eat or don't like before you choose a restaurant.
- Americans often have potluck dinners. This means that everyone brings a large dish to share.

TIPPING

- In the US, the normal amount to tip in a restaurant is about 15%, but 20% is common in a very good restaurant. You don't have to tip in fast-food or self-service restaurants. For groups of six people or more, restaurants sometimes add the tip to the bill.
- It is common to tip taxi drivers about 15%.
- In hotels, tip car valets and bellhops $2.00 to $3.00.

1	People often kiss each other on the cheek when they meet.	True / False
2	You can use a title with a first name, for example, Mr. John.	True / False
3	You shouldn't accept an invitation if you don't plan to go.	True / False
4	It isn't important to arrive on time to an informal party.	True / False
5	It is common for Americans to share a restaurant bill.	True / False
6	At a potluck dinner, you should only eat the food you bring.	True / False
7	Most Americans tip about 10% in restaurants.	True / False
8	Americans usually tip taxi drivers.	True / False

B **IN PAIRS** **An American friend is coming to study in your country. Read the email and discuss answers to his questions.**

New Message

From: jefftheexplorer@usanett.us

To: abl4519@yourcountry.net Cc Bcc

Subject: Social Customs

Wow, I'm going to study in your country! Could you give me some information about social customs? I have a lot of questions!

- Do people usually shake hands when they meet for the first time?
- Do friends kiss on the cheek when they greet each other?
- If I go to someone's house, should I take a gift?
- If I go to someone's house, should I arrive early, on time, or a little late?
- If someone asks me to go to a restaurant, do they pay, or do we share the bill?
- When do people usually leave tips, and how much?

Can you let me know about any other important customs? I don't want to make mistakes!
Thanks for your help!

Jeff

Send

C **IN PAIRS** **Make notes about any other important customs in your country. Use the ideas below or your own ideas.**

- business meetings
- dating
- gift giving
- holidays

____

____

____

D **IN GROUPS** **Discuss the customs that you made notes about in C and give more information. Discuss any points of disagreement.**

We made notes about ordering in a restaurant. First, we ask what everyone likes or doesn't like. Then each person orders one dish and we share all the dishes with everyone.

E **Discuss the questions.**

1 Did members of your group describe the customs and explain what to do clearly? Why or why not?
2 In what other situations do you need to understand differences in customs?

MAKE IT DIGITAL

Find out about a social custom in an English-speaking country. Write about it and post it on your school's website.

VOCABULARY review

SCORE: / 10

A Complete the sentences with the words from the box.

buffet	dressed up	suggestion	reception	show up
checked in	flight	picked up	reservation	wedding

My best friend got married last weekend, and I went to his **1** ______________. My **2** ______________ to Houston arrived at 3:00 and I went to my hotel. The hotel found my **3** ______________ and I **4** ______________ to my room. I had to hurry because the wedding was at 5:00, and I didn't want to **5** ______________ late! I **6** ______________ in my best clothes. My friends from Houston **7** ______________ me ______________ at the hotel and we arrived a little before the ceremony started. The **8** ______________ was in the same place as the ceremony, and it was a lot of fun. The food was fantastic, but I'm going to make a **9** ______________—if you go to a big wedding, arrive for the **10** ______________ early, because the best food disappears fast!

GRAMMAR review

SCORE: / 10

A Choose the correct modal auxiliary.

Sara: I think the math test tomorrow **1 will / would** be really difficult.
Robert: I'm pretty good at math. **2 I may / I'll** help you study if you want.
Sara: Great, thanks! **3 May / Will** I look at your class notes?
Robert: Sure. **4 I'll / I may** come to your house about 5:00 this evening, OK?
Sara: Great. **5 May / Could** you bring your laptop?
Robert: Sure. See you later.

B Decide what Sara and Robert are communicating in A. Then write *R* (request), *PR* (prediction), *I* (intention), *O* (offer), or *PE* (permission).

1 ______________ **2** ______________ **3** ______________ **4** ______________ **5** ______________

16–20 correct: You can make suggestions and talk about wedding ceremonies. You can use modals of intention, offer, prediction, request, and permission.
0–15 correct: Look again at the Vocabulary and Grammar sections in the unit.

TOTAL SCORE: / 20

WHAT DO YOU KNOW NOW? Look back at page 47 and add the words you know now to the box.

STUDY SKILLS ORGANIZING TO HELP MEMORIZATION

Take the quiz. Then go to **Study Skills** on page 131 and learn more about organizing to help memorization.

1 Which do you find easiest to memorize? Rank in order of 1 (very easy) to 6 (very hard).

_____ one word
_____ one word with a picture
_____ a two-word phrase
_____ an underlined word in a sentence
_____ a group of sentences that make a story about a word
_____ a word with a translation

2 Check the techniques that help you memorize new information.

☐ make a song about the thing you want to learn
☐ connect ideas using a story
☐ draw a picture / use color

UNIT 6 Changes

WHAT DO YOU ALREADY KNOW?

1 List five changes in your life in the last year. Include positive and negative changes.

2 IN PAIRS Share and compare your changes. Add more words to your lists.

Changes

VIDEO

DISCUSS & SHARE

3 IN GROUPS Watch the video and answer the question.

SYM Do you view change as a positive or negative thing in your life?

In this unit, you will ...

- talk about risk and change, experiences you want to have, and changes in a city over time.
- use thinking skills: analyze, create, and understand.
- read about how people view change in their lives.
- use strategies to start and keep talking by reacting to information or expressing a point of view.
- use collaboration skills to create a list of recommendations for visitors discovering your town.
- follow an interior designer to learn about this job and the skills needed for the field of architecture.

Change or Stay the Same?

READING

A Choose the answers that are correct for you.

I usually prefer to …

1 eat at the same / different restaurants.
2 eat the same / different foods.
3 go out to the same / different places.
4 listen to the same / new music.
5 go to the same / different places on vacation.

MAKE IT YOURS

Think of other situations in which you usually prefer to do the same thing or usually prefer to do different things.

B 6.01 Read the article. Do Joe and Elena have the same opinion about changes in their lives?

THE STATUS QUO BIAS—

Why People Don't Like Change!

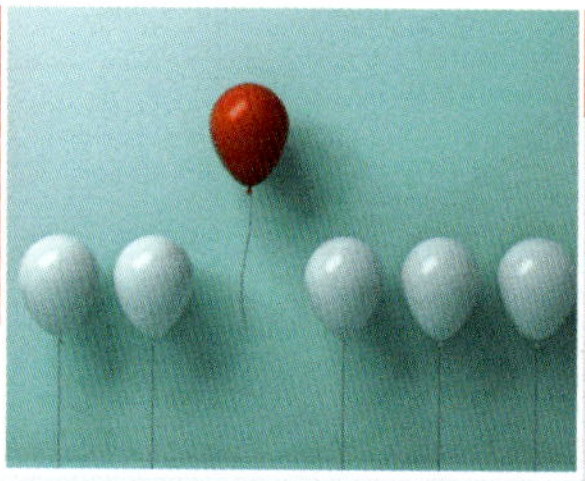

If you prefer the status quo, you don't like change. You prefer things to stay the same. Psychologists call this the **status quo** bias. Many people have a status quo bias, but some people really like change.

Joe and Elena are both 35 years old, but they have very different **attitudes** about change. Joe has lived in the same city, in the same apartment since 2005. He has been with the same company for 12 years. He hasn't bought a new phone for five years, and he has had his car since 2010. Elena has moved three times in the past two years, and she has had four different jobs since 2012. She has worked in her current job for two years, but she thinks she'll probably look for a new job next year.

There are some **advantages** to the status quo. Life is less stressful in your **comfort zone**. You feel that you are **in control** because everything is familiar. There are no **risks**!

However, it can be a good idea to leave your comfort zone and take some risks. This can help you in your professional and personal life. How long have you had the same job? Are there other jobs that pay better or are more interesting? Do you sometimes feel bored with your living situation or your social life? How many times have you eaten at the same restaurant, listened to the same music, gone to the same places on the weekend? If the answer is "a lot," try making a few small changes. Go ahead, order something different the next time you go to that restaurant!

C READING SKILL—Identify examples Read the article in B again. Underline examples that show the following things:

1 the fact that Joe prefers the status quo
2 the fact that Elena prefers change
3 advantages to the status quo
4 a suggestion for a small change

D THINKING SKILL—Analyze Do you think the writer is more in favor of change or the status quo? Use your ability to infer and explain why.

VOCABULARY

A Match the words from the box to the definitions.

advantage attitude comfort zone in control risk status quo

1 ____________: the present situation, or the way things usually are
2 ____________: a situation or place that you feel good in
3 ____________: a positive characteristic of something
4 ____________: the possibility that something bad or dangerous will happen
5 ____________: your opinions or feelings about something
6 ____________: the ability to make decisions and decide what will happen

GRAMMAR present perfect with *for* and *since*

A Read the sentences and choose the correct answer to complete the rules.

Joe has lived in the same city in the same apartment since 2005.
He has been with the same company for 12 years.
How long have you had the same job?

1 The present perfect with *How long*, *for*, and *since* refers to …
- **a** actions or situations that began in the past and continue in the present.
- **b** finished actions or situations.

2 *For* is used with …
- **a** a specific point in time.
- **b** a period of time.

3 *Since* is used with …
- **a** a specific point in time.
- **b** a period of time.

4 *How long* means the same thing as …
- **a** *How much time.*
- **b** *When.*

5 The present perfect is formed with *have/has* and the … of the main verb.
- **a** simple past form
- **b** past participle form

For more practice, go to page 149.

B Use *How long* and the cues to write questions.

1. your family / live in this area? ____________________
2. you / live in your house? ____________________
3. you / know your best friend? ____________________
4. you / study English? ____________________
5. you / have your cell phone? ____________________

PRONUNCIATION present perfect contractions

A 6.02 Listen and repeat. Pay attention to the pronunciation of the contractions with *have* and *has*.

1. I've studied English for several years.
2. You've been here since four o'clock.
3. She's lived here since November.
4. It's been very hot outside for two weeks.
5. We've been in class for 45 minutes.
6. They've worked here for a long time.

B IN PAIRS Practice reading the sentences from A aloud. Remember to stress the main verb, not the contraction with *have*.

SPEAKING

A Answer the questions from GRAMMAR B in your notebook. Then think of more questions to ask a partner.

B IN GROUPS Ask each other the questions you answered in A and the new questions you and your partner wrote. Use the Confident Communicator box to help you. Who likes change and who doesn't like change?

CONFIDENT COMMUNICATOR
KEEP TALKING

Use the following words to talk about periods of time.
For exact amounts of time, use *for six hours, days, months, years.*
For inexact amounts of time, use *about/almost/around/more or less six hours, days, months, years.*

Bucket List

LISTENING

A **Write down four experiences that you would like to have in your life. Tell the class. Find out if anyone in the class has done the things you want to do.**

B 6.03 **Listen to the first part of a podcast. Check (✓) the activities that the speakers want to do.**

- ☐ run a marathon
- ☐ go to Washington, D.C.
- ☐ sing at an open-mic session
- ☐ fly in a helicopter
- ☐ drive a sports car
- ☐ act in a play
- ☐ go snow skiing
- ☐ go bungee jumping
- ☐ ride a motorcycle

C 6.04 **LISTENING SKILL—Listen for main ideas** **Listen to the second part of the podcast. Number the sentences in the correct order. Then underline the two main ideas.**

_____ Your list should include things that you think are possible.
_____ First, try to be realistic.
_____ Thanks for listening, and good luck with your bucket list!
_____ OK, I have a couple of tips for making a bucket list.
_____ Next, don't include too many things on your list.
_____ You probably won't have time to do all of the things on a very long list.

D **THINKING SKILL—Create** **Write two big things and two smaller things for your personal bucket list. Share your ideas with a partner. Give reasons for your choices.**

VOCABULARY life experiences

A **Complete the paragraph with the past participles of verbs from the box.**

be	do	eat	go	hear	meet	ride	run	sing	win

New Message

To: john2397@outmail.cc Cc Bcc

Subject: Bucket list

Hey, John. I like your idea of making a bucket list. There are a lot of things that I've never **1** _____________. First, I've never **2** _____________ my cousins in Spain, and I've never **3** _____________ to the capital of my country. Those are the big things on my list. There are a few smaller things. I've never **4** _____________ camping or **5** _____________ a horse. Let's see … I've never **6** _____________ Korean food, and I've **7** _____________ that it's really good. I like to sing, but I've never **8** _____________ in public. I've **9** _____________ in a few races, but I've never **10** _____________ a race, so I'd like to do that. I guess that's it. What's on your bucket list?

Send

B **IN PAIRS** **Discuss which of the things in the email in A you have done.**

GRAMMAR present perfect with *ever* and *never*

A Read the sentences and choose the correct option to complete the grammar rules.

Have you ever flown in a helicopter? Yes, I have. / No, I haven't.
I've never driven a sports car.

1 *Ever* and *never* refer to actions …
  a at a specific time in the past.
  b at an unspecific time in the past.

2 *Ever* is used in …
  a statements.
  b questions.

3 *Never* is used with …
  a an affirmative verb.
  b a negative verb.

4 In short answers to *yes/no* questions, use …
  a the main verb.
  b *have* or *has*.

For more practice, go to page 150.

B Complete the conversations using the present perfect with *ever* and *never*. Then practice the conversations with a partner.

1 A: Have you ______ driven a sports car?
  B: Yes, I ______.

2 A: ______ your brother ever ______ to Canada?
  B: No, he ______, but he's ______ to the US.

3 A: I ______ never ______ an exotic food. Have you?
  B: Yes, I ______. I ______ eaten snake meat.

4 A: ______ you ______ gone rock climbing?
  B: Yes, I ______. It's scary!

SPEAKING

A Complete the questionnaire for you.

Have you ever …	You	Student 1	Student 2
1 ridden a motorcycle or a horse?			
2 been to another country?			
3 made a video and posted it online?			
4 won a competition or a prize?			
5 flown in a plane?			

B IN GROUPS Talk to two different classmates. Complete the questionnaire in A for them. Ask more questions if you want to. Use the Confident Communicator box to help you.

CONFIDENT COMMUNICATOR
KEEP TALKING

To react to information in a conversation, use the following phrases:
Wow! / Really? That's interesting / awesome / really cool!
You've never done that? / You've done that?
I can't believe it!

VOCABULARY changing cities

A Match the words from the box to the pictures.

bike lane	green space	pedestrian area	shopping mall
food truck	high-rise building	playground	walking trail

1 
______

2 
______

3 
______

4 
______

5 
______

6 
______

7 
______

8 
______

B **IN PAIRS** Which of the features from A are in your area? Discuss.

There are a lot of green spaces, but there aren't many walking trails.

LISTENING

A Look at old and new pictures of Pittsburgh, Pennsylvania. Then answer the question: In what ways do you think the city has changed since the 1970s?

______

______

B 6.05 **LISTENING SKILL—Listen for specific information** **Listen to the radio show *Changing Cities*. Check (✓) the changes to Pittsburgh that Amy mentions.**

They've …

- [ ] built new factories.
- [ ] cleaned up the city.
- [ ] created green spaces.
- [ ] built new high-rise buildings.
- [ ] made walking trails.
- [ ] put in playgrounds.
- [ ] put in pedestrian areas.
- [ ] created bike lanes.

C 6.05 **THINKING SKILL—Understand** **Listen again. Then write one or two sentences that summarize Amy's opinion of Pittsburgh in the 1970s and her opinion now.**

____

____

MAKE IT YOURS

Make a list of words to describe other features of your city or town.

WRITING

A **Read the letter to the editor. Decide whether the writer thinks the changes to his city have been positive or negative. Underline examples that support his opinion.**

LETTER TO THE EDITOR

Our city has seen a lot of changes in the past 10 years. Some of the changes have been good. The city government has repaired many streets, and they've built new bridges. They've also built a new school and a new hospital.

However, there have been a lot of negative changes. They've destroyed several parks and have built high-rise buildings there. They've built large apartment buildings and condominiums in several neighborhoods, and now the traffic is terrible in those areas. They've taken out a lot of bike lanes, and now we can't ride our bikes on those streets. Finally, they've banned food trucks in the city center, so now there are fewer places to eat lunch downtown.

B **Think about the changes in your town. Have the changes been positive or negative?**

C **Write about changes in your town or city in your notebook. Remember to include several examples to support your opinion.**

SPEAKING

A **IN PAIRS** **Create a combined list of changes to your town and their effects. Use the text you wrote in WRITING C to help you. Decide which changes have been positive and which have been negative.**

B **IN GROUPS** **Discuss whether the changes to your town or city have been generally positive or negative. If there is disagreement, try to convince your group to agree with you. Use the Confident Communicator box to help you.**

CONFIDENT COMMUNICATOR
KEEP TALKING

Use these phrases to argue your point of view.

It's true that …, but the fact / problem is that …

The city has built / made / created …, and the effect is that …

That's true, but a positive / negative effect is …

Yes, but on the other hand, …

Language and Life

Collaboration – Recommendations for Your Town

A **6.06 Read the article. According to the writer, what does it mean to be a tourist in your own town?**

GUEST OPINION

Tourist in Your Own Town

By Lynn Williams

I have decided to become a tourist in my own town and the areas near my town. I read an article that said that many people do not know their own towns, and I thought, "That's me!" I've lived here for 15 years, but I always do the same things and go to the same places. I did some research about activities and places in and near my town, and I've made a list of things that I've never done, or that I haven't done in a long time:

- I've never gone to a high school sports event.
- I've been to the history museum only once, several years ago.
- I've never seen the sunset from Pine Mountain.
- There are about 20 restaurants that I've never tried.
- I've never shopped in the farmer's market.
- I haven't taken a walk on the trail next to the river in five years.

Those are only a few of the things on my list. I imagine that it's the same for almost everyone. We all have our routines, and we never do or see a lot of the fun, interesting things near us. So start a sentence with "I've never …" and see how many ways you can complete it. Do some research to find out what there is to do and see in your area. Then, go out and become a tourist in your own town!

B **Choose *True*, *False*, or *NI* (no information).**

1	The writer has lived in her town for a short amount of time.	True / False / NI
2	She travels to other countries frequently.	True / False / NI
3	She thinks there are many interesting things to do in her town.	True / False / NI
4	She hasn't visited the history museum recently.	True / False / NI
5	She has visited other museums in the area.	True / False / NI
6	She thinks most people know a lot about their towns.	True / False / NI

C Make a list of things that you've never done in your town, or haven't done for a long time.

I've never been to a high school soccer game.

I haven't gone to the history museum in years.

D **IN PAIRS** Discuss your lists. Get ideas from your partner to add things to your list.

A: I've never been to a high school soccer game.

B: You haven't? It's lots of fun. My cousin is on the team, so I go to all of the games.

A: Cool. Have you ever been to the history museum?

B: Yes, but I haven't been for about 10 years. It was really interesting, so I'd like to go again.

A: Me, too. I think they've expanded the museum and put in a lot of new exhibits.

E **IN GROUPS** Look at the ideas on your lists and make recommendations for different types of tourists. Try to think of at least two things to do or see for each type of person.

Teenagers	Families with young children
Young people on a date	Senior citizens

F As a class, make a combined list of things that you, your family, and your friends can do in your area that you've never done.

G Discuss the questions.

1 Did you successfully match different types of tourists with activities they might like?
2 In what other situations do you collaborate with others to make recommendations?

MAKE IT DIGITAL

Research interesting activities and places in your area. Post suggestions on your school website or social media site.

VOCABULARY review

SCORE: / 10

A Choose the correct option.

Many people do not like to take **1 risks / advantage**. They prefer to stay in their **2 comfort zones / attitudes** because they like **3 the status quo / risk**. There are people who have never **4 gone / eaten** at a food truck, **5 sung / written** karaoke, or **6 ridden / flown** in an airplane. What about you? Have you ever ridden in a **7 bike lane / pedestrian area** on a busy street or **8 driven / ridden** a horse? Have you ever **9 done / gone** camping or **10 won / met** a competition? If not, try something different!

GRAMMAR review

SCORE: / 10

A Complete the sentences with *for*, *since*, *ever*, *never*, or the correct form of the verb in parentheses.

Di: Hey, have you **1** ____________ (see) the new exhibit at the art museum yet?

Jay: No, I **2** ____________ (have, not). In fact, I've **3** ____________ been to the museum.

Di: Seriously? How long have you **4** ____________ (live) here?

Jay: **5** ____________ I was about 10.

Di: You've **6** ____________ (be) here **7** ____________ 10 years, and you haven't been to the museum?

Jay: Well, I've **8** ____________ liked art museums very much.

Di: Have you **9** ____________ (visit) any of our museums? There are several good ones here.

Jay: Yes, I have, but not **10** ____________ a long time, I guess.

16–20 correct: You can talk about life experiences and changing cities. You can use present perfect with *for, since, ever,* and *never.*
0–15 correct: Look again at the Vocabulary and Grammar sections in the unit.

TOTAL SCORE: / 20

WHAT DO YOU KNOW NOW? Look back at page 57 and add words you know now to the box.

FOLLOW A PRO ARCHITECTURE

Take the quiz about architecture. Then go to Follow A Pro on page 132. Find the answers and learn about the field of architecture.

1 **The word architect comes from the … word *architektōn* meaning "master builder".**
a Latin **b** Old English **c** Greek

2 **The architect Sir Christopher Wren became famous when he designed multiple buildings after London was destroyed by…**
a floods. **b** fire. **c** earthquakes.

3 **From 1912 to 1948, architects could win gold medals at the …**
a Olympics. **b** Masters Tournament. **c** World Cup.

4 **How many years does the typical bachelor's degree in architecture last in the US?**
a 3 **b** 4 **c** 5

UNIT 1

STUDY SKILLS

A Read the two texts. Which is a personal narrative? Which is a factual account?

USING PERSONAL EXPERIENCE

1

Biggest Storm in 100 Years Hits the Country

Yesterday, strong winds of 100 kilometers per hour hit a popular coastal town. Businesses closed early, and buses and trains stopped running. By three p.m. yesterday afternoon, the streets were empty as people stayed inside. Hospitals, however, were very busy as over 100 people were injured by falling trees and flying debris. Luckily, no one was killed.

Sixty centimeters of rain fell in just 24 hours. Streets became rivers, and around 350 people had to leave their homes. Many buildings were damaged by the wind.

An estimated $25 million dollars will be required to repair the damage caused by this storm.

2

An Incredible Storm

I was on a camping trip with some friends. We were hiking in the state park when suddenly there was a huge storm. The sky turned black, and the wind became very strong. We started to feel really scared because we were far from the campground, and no one knew exactly where we were. We hiked back to the start of the trail, but it was really dangerous. Tree branches were breaking, and they almost hit us as they flew. When we arrived at the campground, there was no power, and there was water in the tent. Luckily, we found a hotel for the night. We were happy to be out of the storm!

B How can you tell factual accounts from personal narratives? Write *FA* (factual accounts) or *PN* (personal narratives).

1 _____ use words that describe feelings.
2 _____ often use the passive voice, e.g.: "Many homes were damaged."
3 _____ often use numbers, measurements, and percentages.
4 _____ usually tell stories.
5 _____ are objective.

C Match the columns to make sentences. What effect does it have when you combine fact and personal experience?

1 The earthquake of 2010 left 350,000 people homeless, _____
2 When the biggest music festival in the county took place, _____
3 At 4,810 meters, Mont Blanc is the highest mountain in Europe; _____
4 I think that Tokyo is one of the most exciting cities in the world, _____

a I was there, along with 500,000 other music lovers.
b and with a population of over 37 million, it's also the biggest.
c it is also the place where I learned to ski.
d including my mom, my dad, my brother, and me.

D In your notebook, combine the personal narrative and the factual account from A. Write a paragraph of about 100–125 words.

Remember:
- Don't overdo it. Two to three facts should be enough for a personal narrative.
- Choose the facts you add carefully. Use them only if they add impact to your writing.

When the biggest storm in 100 years hit the coastal area, I was hiking with my friends in the state park. We ...

E THINKING SKILL—Analyze Where do you usually read personal accounts? Where do you usually read factual accounts? Which type of story is more interesting to you? Which is more truthful? Why?

MAKE IT HAPPEN

Think of an exciting experience you have had. Write a paragraph about it, combining facts and personal experience.

Answers to the quiz on page 16
1 b and c 2 a 3 a and b

UNIT 2 FOLLOW A PRO

A **Read about a hotel manager's job. Answer the questions below.**

A HOTEL MANAGER

Albert Chaparro is the hotel manager for a large chain hotel in Lima, Peru. After graduating with a degree in business administration, he joined the chain's graduate training program. There, he learned how to apply his general business skills to the hospitality industry.

His role involves a wide range of activities. He might solve problems with the staff or check hotel supplies. He plays an important role in hiring and training staff, so he might interview applicants or train new workers. He has to manage both people and money.

His job also involves hotel services. He might arrange a large celebration for a group of business visitors. For this, he needs to work closely with the kitchen staff, in particular the head chef. They have to agree on a menu and a budget. During an important event, he monitors wait staff and makes sure everything runs according to plan.

He expects to continue in this job for a few more years. He hopes to get a higher position in hotel management, running a number of hotels in the same chain.

1 What did Albert study before training in hotel management? ______
2 What does Albert do with members of staff? ______
3 Who does Albert work closely with when arranging a celebration? ______
4 When does Albert make sure wait staff are following the plan correctly? ______
5 What does Albert expect to be doing in a few years? ______

B **Discuss the questions as a class.**

1 Do you think Albert's job is interesting? Why or why not?
2 What do you think is the hardest part of Albert's job?

VIDEO

WATCH THE VIDEO AND FOLLOW AN EVENT PLANNER.

C **IN GROUPS Answer the questions.**

1 What job is the video about? ______
2 What does the person do every day? ______
3 Does the person like the job? Why or why not? ______
4 What's the hardest part of the person's job? ______
5 What skills does the person need for the job? ______
6 What education or training did this person have? ______

D **IN GROUPS Check your answers to the quiz on page 24 and discuss the questions.**

1 Do you know people who work in hospitality?
2 What jobs in hospitality do you know?
3 How does knowing English help if you work in hospitality?
4 What personal qualities do you need to work in hospitality?
5 What opportunities to work in hospitality are there where you live?

Answers to the quiz on page 26
1 a 2 c 3 c

UNIT 3

STUDY SKILLS

A A group of students is researching how college students watch entertainment at home. Read the questionnaire they wrote. Are the questions designed well? Why or why not?

DESIGNING A QUESTIONNAIRE

1 Which of the following best describes your job?
Full-time / Part-time

2 How many hours of TV do you watch per day?
Do you prefer series or movies on the internet?
Series / Movies

3 What do you think about reality shows?

4 I prefer to watch TV with friends.
a Strongly agree **b** Agree **c** Neither agree nor disagree
d Disagree **e** Strongly disagree

5 Do you ever lie about how much TV you watch?
Yes / No

B **Read the tips for designing questionnaires. Write the question numbers from A next to all the tips that can improve them. Then underline the questions from the questionnaire in A that follow the tips.**

- **a** Use closed questions that have one answer only. You can count the answers quickly for your research. ______________
- **b** Make sure that your questions ask for just one piece of information. Don't ask two questions at the same time. ______________
- **c** Ask each question the same way. Use all questions or all statements. Write the answer choices in the same way, too. ______________
- **d** Make sure all your questions are on the topic you are researching. ______________
- **e** Make sure your questions don't embarrass or upset the people who might answer them. ______________

C **Rewrite the questionnaire from A in your notebook. Use the tips to help you write good research questions. Write three more well-designed research questions. Ask about the following:**

6 channel surfing: ____?
____

7 binge-watching: ____?
____

8 how they feel about their TV watching habits: ____?
____

D **Write three well-designed survey questions to find out what snacks people eat when they're watching TV.**

E THINKING SKILL—Question **When might you use a questionnaire as part of a job? What jobs depend on getting accurate, useful information from questionnaires?**

MAKE IT HAPPEN

Design a questionnaire for a class, e.g., science, history, geography, or psychology. Decide on a research topic and write four to five questions to research it. Then ask your classmates to answer your questionnaire. Report the results to your class.

Answers to the quiz on page 36
1 a 2 a 3 b
(It's better to ask closed questions.)

UNIT 4 FOLLOW A PRO

A Read about a school psychologist's job. Answer the questions below.

A SCHOOL PSYCHOLOGIST

I'm Laura Cardoso and I work as a school psychologist. I work for the school district in a large city. I have a master's degree, and right now I'm working toward my PhD.

Children have different personalities, abilities, and needs. Most of them do fine in the educational system. However, some children need expert help. Some children find schoolwork hard, while other children are bored because their schoolwork doesn't challenge them enough. A school psychologist works with children to help them with their problems so that they can get the best education possible.

There are two main parts to my job. I work with children, parents, and teachers to plan a learning program for each child that needs help. I try to understand the personalities of the children I work with and any problems they have. I use my training to help them learn. The other part of my job involves training teachers in my city. I travel from school to school and explain common problems children have. It's very motivating to help children do their best.

1 What degree does Laura have? __________
2 Why do some children need a school psychologist? __________
3 Who does Laura work with when planning a learning program? __________
4 What does Laura do besides work with children? __________
5 What does Laura like about her job? __________

B Discuss the questions as a class.

1 Would you like to work as a school psychologist? Why or why not?
2 What skills are important for this job?

VIDEO

WATCH THE VIDEO AND FOLLOW A TEACHER.

C IN GROUPS Answer the questions.

1 What job is the video about? __________
2 Where does the person work? __________
3 Who does the person work with? __________
4 What special education does this person have? __________
5 Is the person happy in this job? __________
6 What does the person say is the best part of the job? __________

D IN GROUPS Check your answers to the quiz on page 44 and discuss the questions.

1 Do you know any people who work in education?
2 What other jobs in education do you know?
3 In what ways might English be useful for a psychologist in the field of education?
4 What personal qualities do you need to work in education?
5 What are the best and worst things about working in education?

Answers to the quiz on page 46
1 c 2 c 3 a

STUDY SKILLS

A Look at the study notes below for one minute. Try to memorize as many words as you can. Then close your book and write what you remember. Was the task hard? Why or why not?

ORGANIZING TO HELP MEMORIZATION

Travel Vocabulary

book a flight
plane
check-in desk
go sightseeing
stay at a campsite
try the local specialties
check in at the airport
baggage claim
rent a vacation home
go through security
airplane
chill out on the beach
bus
take lots of pictures

B Read the tips about organizing your notes for better memorization. Match the memorization tips (1–4) to the examples in the notes (a–d).

1. Organize the words by category. ______
2. Write the words in short phrases. ______
3. Write a short sentence with some of the words. ______
4. Write several sentences that make a story with the words. ______

a *People in a Hotel*	*In the Room*	*Things to Ask the Receptionist*	*Verbs for Hotels*
valet	*king bed / queen bed / twin bed*	*Is breakfast included in the price?*	*book a room*
hotel receptionist	**b** *room with a balcony*	**d** *Can we get some extra towels, please?*	*check into the hotel*
housekeeping	*refrigerator*	*Could you recommend a good restaurant nearby?*	*check out of the hotel*
concierge	**c** *The room in Cancun was perfect. I got a room with a balcony so that I could look at the beach. There was a mini-fridge for snacks, but if I was very hungry, I called room service and ordered lunch.*		*call room service*

C Organize the notes in A so that the words and phrases are easy to remember. Study them for one minute. Then write as many words as you can remember.

Things to Do on Vacation

chill out on the beach

D **THINKING SKILL—Recall** How do you organize information when you need to memorize facts for your classes? Do you organize information in a similar way when you study a language?

MAKE IT HAPPEN

Choose one of the subjects you are studying now. Organize a vocabulary list for that subject so that the words are easier to memorize.

Answers to the quiz on page 56
Students' own answers.

UNIT 6

FOLLOW A PRO

A **Read about the job of an ecological architect. Choose the option that is NOT correct.**

AN ARCHITECT

Emilia Johnson is an architect in a company that specializes in ecological architecture. She completed her bachelor's degree in architecture and environmental design and then got a paid internship with the company. Four years later, she passed the Architect Registration Examination. She has worked at the company for eight years, and she plans to stay there for several more years.

Ecological architects design buildings that are a natural part of the world. They design buildings that use natural resources, such as solar energy. They also design buildings with natural materials, such as a green roof (plants growing on top of a building). Emilia works with civil engineers and interior designers to make sure that her designs have a positive impact on the environment. She explains her designs to urban planners so that her buildings can become part of a larger plan for a city.

Emilia needs good technical skills and creativity. She has to make beautiful buildings that are also water and energy-efficient. She visualizes the design of the project and then creates drawings using CAD (Computer Aided Design) software. She checks that construction workers are following her design.

Emilia loves being an ecological architect. The best part of her job is seeing her clients living and working happily in a building that fits in the world naturally.

1. For four years, Emilia worked **as an intern** / **as a volunteer** / **before passing an exam** / **on ecological buildings**.
2. Ecological architects create buildings with **natural materials** / **solar panels** / **plants** / **plastic roofs**.
3. Emilia's designs are **used by engineers and designers** / **created on computers** / **made by clients** / **explained to urban planners**.
4. Ecological architects need good **marketing** / **communication** / **technical** / **creative** skills.

B **Discuss the questions as a class.**

1. Do you think it is important to create ecological architecture? Why or why not?
2. How can architects help make buildings more ecological?
3. Have you been in any buildings that are "green"? How do those buildings save water or energy?

VIDEO **WATCH THE VIDEO AND FOLLOW AN URBAN PLANNER.**

C **IN GROUPS Answer the questions.**

1. What job is the video about? ______
2. What are the person's working hours? ______
3. What are some of the good and bad things about the job? ______
4. Is the person's job hard? Why or why not? ______
5. What skills does the person use at this job? ______

D **IN GROUPS Check your answers to the quiz on page 64 and discuss the questions.**

1. What other jobs in architecture do you know?
2. Do you need English to be an architect?
3. What personal qualities do you need for this job?
4. Are there opportunities in the field of architecture in your country?

Answers to the quiz on page 66
1 c 2 b 3 a 4 c

Irregular Verbs

Infinitive	Simple past	Past participle
be	was/were	been
become	became	become
begin	began	begun
break	broke	broken
bring	brought	brought
build	built	built
buy	bought	bought
catch	caught	caught
choose	chose	chosen
come	came	come
cost	cost	cost
cut	cut	cut
do	did	done
draw	drew	drawn
drink	drank	drunk
drive	drove	driven
eat	ate	eaten
fall	fell	fallen
feed	fed	fed
feel	felt	felt
find	found	found
fly	flew	flown
get	got	gotten
give	gave	given
go	went	gone
grow	grew	grown
hang	hung	hung
have	had	had
hear	heard	heard
hit	hit	hit
hold	held	held
hurt	hurt	hurt
keep	kept	kept
know	knew	known
leave	left	left
let	let	let
lose	lost	lost
make	made	made
meet	met	met
pay	paid	paid
put	put	put
read	read	read
ride	rode	ridden
ring	rang	rung
rise	rose	risen
run	ran	run
say	said	said
see	saw	seen
sell	sold	sold
send	sent	sent
set	set	set
sing	sang	sung
sit	sat	sat
speak	spoke	spoken
stand	stood	stood
stick	stuck	stuck
take	took	taken
teach	taught	taught
tell	told	told
think	thought	thought
throw	threw	thrown
understand	understood	understood
wake	woke	woken
wear	wore	worn
win	won	won
write	wrote	written

Pronunciation Symbols

Vowels

ɪ	did
ɛ	bed
æ	bad
ʌ	cup
ʊ	book
ə	banana
i	feed
ɑ	father, box
ɔ	tall
u	student, food
ɚ	shirt, birthday
eɪ	date, table
aɪ	cry, eye
ɔɪ	boy
oʊ	comb, post
aʊ	about, how

Consonants

p	park, happy
b	back, hobby
t	tea
d	die
k	came, kitchen, quarter
g	game, go
f	face, photographer
V	vegetable
θ	thing, math
ð	then, that
s	city, summer
z	please, goes
ʃ	she, shop
ʒ	leisure
h	hot, who
tʃ	chicken, watch
dʒ	jacket, orange
m	men
n	sun, know
ŋ	sung, singer
w	week, white
r	rain, writer
l	light, long
j	yes, use, music

Grammar Review

A Match the questions (1–8) to the answers (a–h). Write the letter.

1 Do you like using social media? _____
2 How's it going? _____
3 Who do you live with? _____
4 When do you start work? _____
5 Is there a library in your town? _____
6 Can you run fast? _____
7 How much milk do we have? _____
8 Did he do his homework? _____

a We have half a liter.
b At 9 a.m.
c No, I can't!
d Good, thanks.
e No, there isn't.
f My parents and my brother.
g Yes, I do.
h Yes, he did.

B Complete the sentences with the phrases from the box.

has to | like to | need to | plan to | want to | would like to

1 Next year, I really __________ travel the world.
2 __________ you __________ come with me?
3 I __________ plan my trip before I go.
4 My passport __________ be up to date.
5 I __________ be away for about a year.
6 I __________ travel. It's one of my favorite things.

C Complete simple past sentences using the verbs in parentheses.

1 Last weekend, I __________ (celebrate) my birthday with family and friends.
2 We __________ (go) to my favorite restaurant.
3 I __________ (not have) a party at my home because my apartment is too small.
4 The meal __________ (be) delicious, and we all really __________ (enjoy) it.
5 We __________ (not go) to a movie because it was so late when we finished dinner.
6 What __________ (do) you do last weekend?

D Complete the conversation with the comparative form of the adjectives in parentheses.

Tim: Where do you want to eat this weekend? Do you want to go to the pizza place or the new restaurant?
Lara: Hmm, I don't know. The pizza place is **1** __________ (cheap).
Tim: Yes, but I think the food at the new place is **2** __________ (good). Their salads look good, too. I think you get **3** __________ (healthy) food there.
Lara: You're probably right. I'm not sure about the staff at the new place. I think the waiters at the pizza place are **4** __________ (friendly).
Tim: So many people are talking about the new restaurant, though! It's **5** __________ (popular) than the pizza place.
Lara: Yes, but the pizza place is **6** __________ (close), and it's raining.

E Rewrite the sentences correctly.

1 She can run really fastly. ______________________
2 She speaks English good. ______________________
3 Can you more slowly speak, please? ______________________
4 You need to do very carefully this. ______________________
5 He caught the ball easy. ______________________
6 He studied hardly for his exam. ______________________

F Read and choose the correct option.

I really love my hometown. **1 There are / There is** a lot of nice restaurants and **2 there are / there is** some small cafés, too. **3 There is / There are** a big library, and **4 there's / there are** a school. **5 There aren't / There isn't** too many stores, but there is a beautiful park. What about your town? **6 Are there / Is there** a lot of things to do?

G Complete the sentences with the present progressive form of the words in parentheses.

1 Rory ______________________ (take) a selfie.
2 Sula ______________________ (update) her profile.
3 Jan ______________________ (post) comments on a blog.
4 Manny and Luca ______________________ (send) texts to each other.
5 Mary's video ______________________ (go) viral.
6 Everyone ______________________ (look) at their screens.
7 They ______________________ (not speak) to each other.

H Read and choose the correct option.

Ava: Can I have **1 some / a** milk, please?
Will: Of course. **2 How much / How many** do you want?
Ava: I'd like a liter, please. Can I have **3 this / some** apples, too?
Will: Sure. **4 These / This** red ones?
Ava: No, **5 those / that** green ones, please.
Will: Here you go.
Ava: **6 How much / How many** is that, please?

UNIT 1 — past progressive

Function

We use the past progressive to talk about an action that began in the past and continued for some time.

Form

Affirmative		Negative	
I was	watching TV.	I wasn't	watching TV.
You were	studying English.	You weren't	studying English.
He was She was It was	playing video games. learning the guitar. raining.	He wasn't She wasn't It wasn't	playing video games. learning the guitar. raining.
We were	listening to music.	We weren't	listening to music.
They were	dancing together.	They weren't	dancing together.

Yes/No questions		Affirmative short answer	Negative short answer
Was I	sleeping?	Yes, I was.	No, I wasn't.
Were you	listening?	Yes, you were.	No, you weren't.
Was he Was she Was it	cooking? singing? snowing?	Yes, he was. Yes, she was. Yes, it was.	No, he wasn't. No, she wasn't. No, it wasn't.
Were we	working?	Yes, we were.	No, we weren't.
Were they	running?	Yes, they were.	No, they weren't.

UNIT 1 — past progressive vs. simple past

Function

We use the past progressive to describe an action in progress, and the simple past to introduce an interrupting action.

Form

Action in progress	Interrupting action
I was eating a sandwich	when my phone rang.
We were running a marathon	when it started raining.
She was out shopping	when she met a friend.
Were you watching TV	when you heard the news?

Interrupting action	Action in progress
The fire broke out	while they were sleeping.
The accident happened	while my brother was driving.
When I woke up,	it was raining.
Where were you	while this was happening?

A Read the conversation and choose the correct option.

Marta: What **1 were** / **was** you doing last night? Did you see the match on TV?

Sam: No, I didn't. I **2 was reading** / **read** a book. It was so good I forgot about the match!

Marta: What was the book about?

Sam: It's a biography about an artist in New York. When he was a child, he was always drawing and **3 painted** / **painting**. Then one day, when he was playing in the street, a car **4 hit** / **was hitting** him. He was badly hurt. While he was in the hospital, a nurse **5 gave** / **was giving** him a book about art. This book made him want to become an artist. Then years later, he **6 was drawing** / **drew** in the park when he **7 was seeing** / **saw** the nurse who gave him the book. While they **8 talked** / **were talking**, he drew her a picture to say thank you.

Marta: Wow! I bet that picture's worth millions of dollars now!

B Complete the sentences with the present progressive or the past tense form of the words in parentheses.

1. Anna _______________ (watch) the sunset when she decided to start her own business. The first thing she needed was some money.
2. When she _______________ (call) her bank, the bank manager was speaking to another customer.
3. Anna _______________ (write) her business plan when the bank manager returned her call.
4. While they _______________ (discuss) Anna's idea, her friend Greta came into the room.
5. Greta _______________ (ask) who Anna was talking to.
6. Anna was explaining her business plan to her friend when she _______________ (get) an email from the bank manager saying the bank could lend her the money.

UNIT 2 — quantifiers: *some, any, too much/many, a lot of, a little, a few*

Function

We use quantifiers to talk about amounts. Some quantifiers go with countable nouns, some go with uncountable nouns, and some go with both.

Form

Countable	Uncountable	Both
a few too many	a little too much	some any a lot of

A Identify the mistakes and rewrite the sentences correctly.

1. There's only a few milk in the refrigerator.

   ____

2. I think there's too many salt in this meal.

   ____

3. You need a lot tomatoes to make tomato soup.

   ____

4. Can you please buy me a little apples when you're at the store?

   ____

5. Don't eat too many candy! It's not good for you.

   ____

6. Can I have some grape, please?

   ____

B Choose the correct option.

At the end of winter, **1 a lot of / a little** people around the world celebrate the end of cold, dark days. **2 Some / A little** towns and villages do this by having street parties and making fires. On the Scottish island of Shetland, there is a fire festival every January. At that time of year, it's really cold and there's only **3 a little / a few** daylight. Not **4 too many / too much** people live in Shetland, but the party is huge! I wanted to go to the fire festival last year, but the flights cost **5 too much / too many** money. I'm saving money now, and I plan to go there next year with **6 a few / a little** friends.

UNIT 2 — *enough / not enough*

Function

We use *enough* to show that something is the right amount. *Not enough* shows that something is not the right amount. We use *enough* with countable and uncountable nouns.

Form

Countable	Uncountable
There are enough apples. We don't have enough books. There aren't enough cookies. Not enough people know about it. Do we have enough chairs?	She has enough money. They don't have enough clothes. There is enough milk. There is not enough time to finish the test. Is there enough room?

A Unscramble and write the sentences.

1 enough / this / have / we / do / food / for / party / ?

____

2 I / think / have / enough / we / .

____

3 enough / we / really / do / have / pizza / ?

____

4 enough / we / pizza / have / .

____

5 chairs / there / are / enough / ?

____

6 don't / enough / to / more / chairs / get / we / have / time / !

____

UNIT 3 — indefinite pronouns: *any, some, no, every + one/body/thing/where*

Form and function

We use indefinite pronouns when we are talking about a thing, person, or amount in a nonspecific way.
Use *any–* in questions or negative statements. *I don't want to do anything.*
Any– is used when it's not certain if a person, place, or thing exists. *Is anyone there?*
Any– is also used to refer to all persons, places, or things. *Anyone can do it.*

Indefinite pronoun	Means ...	Example
everything	all things	I love everything about Paris!
everybody	all people	Everybody likes Anna.
everyone	all people	Everyone knows you.
everywhere	all places	They go everywhere together.
nothing	no things	There was nothing in his wallet.
nobody	no people	Nobody told me the news.
no one	no people	No one lives here.
nowhere	no places	This is like nowhere on Earth.
something	an unknown thing	I think I heard something.
somebody	an unknown person	Somebody heard us. Run!
someone	an unknown person	Someone is watching them.
somewhere	an unknown place	I need to go somewhere quiet.
anything	non-specific things	Can you see anything?
anybody	non-specific people	I don't know anybody here!
anyone	non-specific people	There isn't anyone I can ask.
anywhere	non-specific place	Is there anywhere we can go?

A Complete the text with indefinite pronouns from the box.

anyone anyone everyone no one something something

Last summer, I wanted to do **1** ____________ a little different for my vacation. My friends were all away, and there was **2** ____________ to hang out with. **3** ____________ was posting on social media about what a cool time they were having, so I decided to do **4** ____________ cool, too. I joined a summer camp for young people who wanted to learn about the art of street entertaining. At first, I felt nervous because I didn't know **5** ____________ there. After a few days, I loved it. I learned how to juggle and also learned some neat magic tricks. Did **6** ____________ have as good a vacation as I did? I doubt it!

B Identify the mistakes and rewrite the sentences correctly.

1 When I first moved here, I didn't know someone. ____________
2 Anyone seemed to have their own friends, so it was hard to meet people.
____
3 I felt lonely and decided I needed to do anything about it.
____
4 I looked around everything for clubs I could join. ____________
5 Finally, I found anything I was interested in—a video gaming club.
____
6 I really love this club. Someone is so friendly! ____________

UNIT 3 — *used to*

Function

We use *used to* to describe a habitual past action that isn't happening now.

Form

Affirmative			Negative		
I You He/She It We They	used to	live here. do ballet. play football. take a long time. go there. be friends.	I You He/She It We They	didn't use to	like it, but now I love it. recycle, but now you do. exercise, but now he/she runs marathons. work, but I just fixed it. hang out, but now we meet every weekend. play soccer, but now they're good at it.

Questions			
Did	I you he/she it we they	use to	make up songs as a child? work there? go running? play music? go there often? live here?

A Identify the mistakes and rewrite the sentences correctly.

1 Did your brother used to singing in a band? ____________
2 He use to be the lead singer of a hard rock band. ____________
3 I didn't used to like hard rock, but now I love it. ____________
4 Did you used take a music class at school? ____________
5 Yeah, I used taking one, but I stopped! It was a lot of extra work.
____
6 You should try again. There's a different teacher now. The last teacher use to make us work too hard!
____

B Choose the correct option.

1 The café we **used to** / **use to** eat in is now a really cool clothes shop.
2 He **use to** / **didn't use to** wear nice clothes, but now he looks great!
3 I **didn't use to** / **didn't used to** speak English, but now I do.
4 Did they **use to** / **used to** be friends? They don't talk to each other now.
5 My sister **used to** / **use to** be a teacher, but now she's a business owner.
6 He **didn't use to** / **used to** eat fast food all the time, but now he eats very healthily.
7 Did you **use to** / **used to** live here? I think I recognize you from somewhere.

UNIT 4 — comparative review and *(not) as … as*

Function

We use comparatives to compare one thing, person, or place to another thing, person, or place. We use *as … as* to show that two things are equal. We use *(not) as … as* to show that two things are not equal.

Form

Adjectives with one syllable	Adjectives that end with –y and have two syllables
My sister is quieter than I am. Silvia is nicer than Ella.	Horacio is happier than Frank. I'm lazier than my sister is.

Adjectives with two or more syllables	Irregular forms
Cities are more expensive than small towns. He is more handsome than his father. Now I'm more ambitious than I was then.	He's a better cook than his sister is. New York is farther from her than Chicago is.

as … as	(not) as … as
She's as friendly as her daughter. He's as tall as I am. I'm as stressed as you are about this.	I'm not as creative as you are. They're not as hard-working as we are. She's not as optimistic as she used to be.

A Choose the correct option.

My brother and I are twins—we look very similar, except that I'm **1 as tall as / not as tall as** he is. I'm only 175 centimeters! We both have blue eyes, although I think his eyes **2 are bluer / are more bluer**. When it comes to personality, we're really different. I don't think he's **3 as serious as / not as serious as** I am. He's **4 more sociable / sociabler** than I am and likes hanging out with his friends, while I like to be alone. I'd like to be **5 as easygoing / not as easygoing** as he is, but I wouldn't like to be **6 as lazy / not as lazy** as he is!

B Correct the mistakes.

1 I think that the coffee in this café is more good than the other one. ______
2 A city vacation is expensiver than a vacation in the country. ______
3 Our apartment isn't modern as yours. ______
4 Is your homework as hard like mine? ______
5 Her driving isn't getting better. It's getting badder! ______
6 You should do this task first because it's importanter. ______
7 Tom was as happy than you when he heard the news. ______

UNIT 4 — superlative adjectives

Function

We use superlatives to compare more than two things.

Form

Adjectives with one syllable	Adjectives that end with –y and have two syllables
It's the cheapest restaurant in town. What's the quickest way to get there? It's the smallest room in the house.	She's the funniest girl in the class. That was the happiest day of my life. July is the sunniest month in my country.

Adjectives with two or more syllables	Irregular forms
He's the most interesting man I've ever met. I think she's the most confident student. You're the most patient teacher in the school.	This is the best holiday ever! I've had the worst day. I think she ran the farthest.

A Complete the conversation with the superlative form of the adjectives in parentheses.

Sue: I'm organizing the end-of-year awards, Robert. Can you help me?
Robert: Well, I know what you should get the prize for, Sue—**1** ______ (hardworking) student in the school!
Sue: Aw, thanks, Robert! We don't have that category this year, though. There is a prize for **2** ______ (easygoing) person in our grade. Who should that be?
Robert: Hmm, what about Donato? He doesn't really do anything at all. He could win the prize for **3** ______ (lazy) guy, maybe?
Sue: That wouldn't be very nice! I also need to find someone to win the prize for **4** ______ (creative) idea of the year.
Robert: What about Daniella's charity fashion show? That was really creative.
Sue: Ah, yes, good idea. There's also a prize for **5** ______ (good) team worker …
Robert: Oh, that should be Nick. He likes everyone. You know, I really think he's **6** ______ (nice) guy in the whole school.

UNIT 5 — modals of intention, offer, and prediction

Function and form

We use modal verbs *will/won't* to state our intentions, make and refuse offers, and make predictions. We also use *can/can't* to make and refuse offers.

	Intention	Prediction
affirmative	I'll check out at 10 a.m. We'll go sightseeing today.	It'll rain tomorrow! We'll be there in three hours.
negative	I won't stay late. We won't stay here again.	There won't be any free rooms. We won't get there in time.

Make an offer	Refuse an offer
I'll help you with that! Can you stay for dinner? We can go sightseeing today.	No thanks, I won't need help. I can't stay any longer. I can't today, maybe tomorrow.

A Choose the correct option.

Receptionist: Hi, welcome to City Hostel! **1** Can / Will I help you?
Sandor: Hi! My name is Sandor Vargas. I've booked three nights here—but it looks so lovely here that I think **2** I'll / I can stay a little longer.
Receptionist: Great! **3** Will / Won't you extend your reservation by another night, then? **4** I'll / I won't check our availability.
Sandor: Thanks.
Receptionist: That's fine. We **5** will / won't be very busy for the next few nights. It's often quiet at this time of year. So, here's your key card. Breakfast is from 6 to 8 a.m.
Sandor: Great. I'm really tired, so I probably **6** will / won't go to breakfast tomorrow.

B Complete the sentences with words from the box.

can 'll 'll will will won't won't

1 ______________ you come to my birthday party next Friday?
2 It ______________ be easy to study and work part time in the café. It's too much!
3 ______________ I help you carry your bags? They look heavy.
4 I ______________ be a little late getting home today because I have a dentist appointment after school.
5 ______________ you stay and have dinner with us? We're having pizza.
6 She ______________ probably tell you about it the next time she sees you.
7 Rocio and Peter ______________ come to the match on Sunday. They don't really like sports.

UNIT 5 — modals of request and permission: *could, can/can't, may*

Function

We use modals *could*, *can/can't*, and *may* to request and grant permission. We use *can* to ask for permission informally, whereas *may* and *could* are formal and more polite. We use *can't* to refuse permission, *can* to grant permission, and *may* to formally grant permission.

Form

Asking for permission	Granting permission	Refusing permission
Can I use your pencil?	Yes, you can.	You can't borrow my pencil.
Could we borrow your car?	Of course you can borrow my car!	You may not borrow my car.
May we go home now?	Yes, you may.	You may not.
Could I speak to you about that?	Yes, you can.	No, you can't.
May I have your phone number?	Yes, you may. It's …	No, you may not.

A Choose the correct option.

1 **Can I** / **I can** visit you next weekend?
2 No, you **can't** / **can** look at my homework.
3 **May I** / **you** ask your advice about something?
4 Yes, you **may not** / **may**.
5 **May** / **Can** we speak to you after class, Professor?
6 No, you **can't** / **can**.
7 "Could we sit here?" "Yes, you **could** / **can**."

B Unscramble and write the sentences.

1 I / open / can / window / the / ?

____

2 may / see / I / ID / your / ?

____

3 you / yes, / can / use / bike / my / .

____

4 yes, / may / you / now / go / .

____

5 can / address / have / your / I / email / ?

____

6 we / could / juice / more / orange / have / ?

____

UNIT 6 — present perfect with *for* and *since*

Function and form

We use the present perfect with *for* or *since* to talk about actions or situations that began in the past and continue in the present. *For* is used for a period of time, and *since* is used with a specific time. *How long* means *how much time*.

We form the present perfect with the auxiliary *have/has* and the past participle of the verb. With regular verbs, we form the past participle by adding *–ed*. Many verbs have irregular past participles.

Present perfect affirmative	Present perfect negative	Questions with *how long*
I've known her for five years.	I haven't known her for very long.	How long have I known you?
You've had this car for two months.	You haven't had that car for two months.	How long have you worked here?
She's lived here since 2016.	She hasn't lived here since 2016.	How long has it been like this?
He's studied here since January.	We haven't studied here since January.	How long has he felt like that?
We've been married for one year.	We haven't been married for one year.	How long have we driven for?
They've been there for a long time.	They haven't been there for a long time.	How long have they lived together?

A Read and choose the correct option.

1 I've known Maria **for** / **since** we were children.
2 She's been here **for** / **since** a long time.
3 They've driven to work together **for** / **since** years.
4 We've been members of that gym **for** / **since** last July.
5 She's had the same cell phone **for** / **since** two years.
6 I've worked with the same company **for** / **since** 2015.

B Complete the conversation using the prompts in parentheses.

Naomi: I want to do something different with my life. I am bored! **1** ______________________ (I / live) in this area for a long time, and I need a change.
Aaron: Yes, you've been here **2** ______________________ (a long time).
How **3** ______________________ (long / you / have) this job?
Naomi: For about three years!
Aaron: Maybe you should take a vacation and take some time to plan your future. I saw some cheap flights to Greece yesterday. **4** ______________________ (Have you / be / there)?
Naomi: No, I haven't! That's a good idea. **5** ______________________ (I / not / have / vacation / since) last summer.
Aaron: **6** ______________________ (It / be / long time / since) I've had a vacation, actually. I think I need to take a break, too!

UNIT 6 — present perfect with *ever* and *never*

Function

Ever and *never* refer to actions at an unspecific time in the past. *Ever* is used in questions and *never* is used with an affirmative verb.

Form

Questions with ever	Short answers	Never
Have you ever been to Greece? Have you ever ridden a motorcycle? Has she ever traveled the world?	Yes, I have. / No, I haven't. Yes, you have. / No, you haven't. Yes, she has. / No, she hasn't. Yes, we have. / No, we haven't. Yes, they have. / No, they haven't.	I've never been to Greece. I've never ridden a motorcycle. She's never traveled the world.

A Complete the conversation with the words from the box.

been ever have haven't never tried

Ben: I think I'd like to try the new restaurant that's just opened. Have you **1** __________ been there?
Sally: No, I **2** __________, but I've heard it's not very good.
Ben: Oh, really? What about the pizzeria on the main square? Have you ever **3** __________ it?
Sally: Yes, I **4** __________. I went there just last week. It's amazing; you should try it!
Ben: I think I will. My cousin's coming to visit this weekend. He's never **5** __________ here before, so I want to show him all the sights!
Sally: Is that your cousin from the US? I've **6** __________ met him before. You should introduce us!

B Match the halves to make sentences.

1 I've never eaten ____
2 Have you ever cooked ____
3 She's never been ____
4 They've never met before, ____
5 Have you ever swum ____
6 We've never traveled ____

a to my house, so I gave her directions.
b in the Atlantic Ocean?
c by plane, so we're a little nervous.
d but I think they'll like each other.
e Mexican food, but I want to try it.
f a meal for a big group of people?

Unit 1

Track 01

Lila Downs

My role model is Lila Downs. She was born in Oaxaca, Mexico, in 1968. She is a Mexican-American singer-songwriter and actress. At the age of eight, she started singing mariachi songs. She became a professional singer when she was at school. Her family emigrated from Mexico to the US when she was 14. While they were living there, her father died. After that, Lila and her mother moved back to Mexico.

While she was working in her mother's store, she met her future husband, the musician Paul Cohen. He had a business in the US, so Lila moved from Oaxaca to Minnesota. She went to the University of Minnesota. While she was studying there, she started a music group called La Trova Serrana. It was very successful, and Lila decided to leave school to focus on music. Lila had a small role in the movie *Frida* and worked on the music for the movie *Like Water for Chocolate*.

Here are three things you probably don't know about Lila:

- In 2010, while she was traveling the world on her Black Magic Woman Tour, she revealed that she had an adopted son named Benito Dxuladi.
- In 2014, scientists named an insect after her. The Liladownsia fraile is a very colorful grasshopper. They named it after her because Lila often wears colorful, traditional clothes.
- She sings in Spanish, English, and her native language of Mixtec.

I really look up to Lila Downs because she looks for ways to improve people's lives through music. I'd love to meet her and ask her this question: "What were you singing about in the song 'Shake Away'?"

Track 02

Host: We asked four people to tell us about memorable events. Here's what they said.

Katrin: I remember we were walking downtown to buy groceries. Suddenly, a police officer shouted, "Hide!" We hid in a café. A man said wild animals escaped from a zoo. I don't remember feeling scared. I think I was worried that they would kill the animals. Luckily, they caught the animals!

Giovanni: I was watching the game at my friend's house when the phone rang. It was my mom. She said my wife was having the baby! I raced to the hospital. We lost the game 2–1, so it was the end of our World Cup, but that wasn't important. I was so thrilled about the new baby!

Kyle: I was working for NASA on the Mars mission when it happened. My boss called me in the middle of the night while I was sleeping, so I was very confused. "The Italians found an underground lake on Mars," he shouted.

Gemma: When the plane came down, we were staying in a hotel. I turned on the TV, and what I saw was unbelievable. All the people were standing on the wings of the plane. I was so glad that everyone was OK. I decided to train to become a pilot after that.

Track 03

Katrin: Suddenly a police officer shouted, "Hide!" We hid in a café.

Track 04

1	hid	hide	**3**	mad	made
2	at	ate	**4**	rid	ride

Track 05

About two years ago, my cousin was walking home when he saw a woman. He thought it was me.

A month later, my friend said, "I saw you in the library last week."

"But I was on vacation in Hawaii last week!" I said.

About a month after that, I was shopping for food when a woman came up to me. I looked at her and … well, she looked exactly like me–same hair color, same eyes, same everything!

Track 06

While I was talking to her, I thought we might be related. She said she was an only child. She was adopted when she was two and lived in San Diego until she was 18. Her parents divorced when she was eight. She is engaged to a guy from Australia.

I said I lived in Los Angeles until I was 12. I told her I was single and came from a large family. I have seven brothers and sisters. We were laughing about how we looked the same, but how we had very different lives. Anyway, we exchanged phone numbers and said goodbye. Later on, I called my mom to check if I had a twin sister! She said I didn't.

The next day, I called the woman, and we agreed to meet for coffee. We see each other all the time now. I'm so glad I met her. In the end, she became one of my best friends. It was such an amazing coincidence that we met!

Track 07

About two years ago, my cousin was walking home when he saw a woman. He thought it was me.

A month later, my friend said, "I saw you in the library last week."

"But I was on vacation in Hawaii last week!" I said.

About a month after that, I was shopping for food when a woman came up to me. I looked at her and … well, she looked exactly like me—same hair color, same eyes, same everything!

While I was talking to her, I thought we might be related. She said she was an only child. She was adopted when she was two and lived in San Diego until she was 18. Her parents divorced when she was eight. She is engaged to a guy from Australia.

I said I lived in Los Angeles until I was 12. I told her I was single and came from a large family. I have seven brothers and sisters. We were laughing about how we looked the same, but how we had very different lives. Anyway, we exchanged phone numbers and said goodbye. Later on, I called my mom to check if I had a twin sister! She said I didn't.

The next day, I called the woman, and we agreed to meet for coffee. We see each other all the time now. I'm so glad I met her. In the end, she became one of my best friends. It was such an amazing coincidence that we met!

Track 08

Victor Karlsson

Meet 20-year-old Victor Karlsson from Malmo, Sweden. When Victor was eight years old, he became blind in an accident. With help from his family and friends, Victor is now a local hero in Malmo. Victor and his guide dog Charlie are helping improve the lives of blind children and adults by raising money. In 2018, Victor raised 1,500 euros walking 111 km between Malmo and Copenhagen. In 2020, he is planning to run a half-marathon. "Everyone looks up to Victor," says his friend Katya. "He's a true role model."

Petra Gonzales

Nineteen-year-old Petra Gonzales saved her sister from a fire in their home in Mexico. Petra, a university student, woke up one night to the smell of smoke. She woke up her sister. She was carrying her sister out of their apartment when she saw the fire on the other side of the house. Amazingly, firefighters arrived in time to save both girls. Petra got an award from the local mayor. "I was really scared," said Petra, "but I was just doing what any sister would do."

Mimi Kallas

While Mimi Kallas was working in a tourist office in her home town in Greece, she noticed men and women on the streets asking for food. Mimi stopped working at her job and started a food service for homeless people. She collects extra food from stores and cooks up to 100 meals a day in the kitchen of a school. She gives out the food for free to anyone who needs it. "Without Mimi, we couldn't survive," said one man. "She is an amazing woman. I'm so glad she is here to help us."

Unit 2

Track 01

Every Day is a Holiday!

Take a look at your calendar for the year ahead. Some dates show an official event that people celebrate somewhere in the world. For example, Americans celebrate Independence Day on July 4. On October 8, the Japanese celebrate Health and Sports Day. A lot of people get the day off work, and schools and businesses are closed. People may eat special food on these days or give and receive gifts.

Then there are unofficial holidays. These are days when people sometimes arrange a party at school or at work. Unofficial holidays celebrate unimportant and fun things like food, movies, books, and TV shows.

To show you what I mean, last week, a colleague said, "It's 'Take a Selfie Day'! Today you can take a lot of selfies." In my opinion, there's too much time spent taking selfies—you don't need a special day for it!

There are a few websites that list all these celebrations. Think of any day of the year, and there is something to celebrate. I learned there are days of the year for everything: Read in the Bathtub Day (February 9), World Yoga Day (February 22), and my favorite, Make Music Day (June 21). A lot of days celebrate food, like Caesar Salad Day on July 4 and Eat a Peach Day on August 22. There are too many dates for me to remember!

I am thinking of asking my boss if I can get the day off on the second Friday of March. It's World Sleep Day. And a little advice for you—don't think of asking me to do anything on Lazy Day (August 10)!

Track 02

Jen: Do you know what I don't like?
Will: What?
Jen: Commercialization.
Will: What do you mean?
Jen: Well, it's when businesses use celebrations to make money. For example, all the things for Valentine's Day—decorations, candy, cards—are in stores in January, when the holiday is in February!
Will: And Halloween stuff is in stores in September, when the holiday is in October.
Jen: I have enough decorations. I don't need to spend money on new ones every year. It's easy to overspend.
Will: Some people waste money on crazy costumes for Halloween. One hundred dollars for a monster costume! That's too much money!
Jen: Yeah! I found a great Halloween costume for $15 online. You can find cheaper things if you shop around.
Will: That's true. I don't like commercialization. I know a few families who borrow money to pay for gifts at Christmas. They don't have enough money but feel like they have to buy things.
Jen: That's too bad. Celebrations should be a time for rest and relaxation, not stress and buying.

Track 03

Before I start cooking, I'd like to tell you a little bit about dumplings because they're a very important part of the celebration. It's traditional for families all over China to sit down together at midnight to eat them. In fact, they say that the person who eats the most dumplings will have good luck throughout the whole year!

Track 04

There are different types of dumplings, but I'm going to show you how to make fried vegetarian dumplings with mushrooms, water chestnuts, and green onions.

So for the outside of the dumplings, you will need two packages of dumpling wrappers. You can find these in Chinese markets or get them online.

Next, you need the ingredients for the inside: one can of water chestnuts, one bag of green onions, two boxes of mushrooms, and two teaspoons of Chinese spices. You also need garlic and a small bottle of oil for frying.

Now let's start cooking. Chop the water chestnuts, green onions, garlic, and mushrooms. Fry them in a little oil. Add the Chinese spices and stir. Cook for about 10 minutes until the mushrooms are soft.

Now let's wrap the dumplings. Put the dumpling wrappers in some water for 30 seconds, until they're soft. Take a little mushroom mix and put it in the center of the wrapper. Don't add too much. Fold over the edge of the wrapper and press. There you go! You should get about 30 dumplings. Fry them for a few minutes on each side.

You can also make a delicious sauce with one jar of sweet chili sauce, sesame seeds, chopped ginger, and half a bottle of soy sauce.

There you go–my delicious Chinese New Year dumplings!

Track 05

1 shop chop
2 ships chips
3 sheep cheap

Track 06

Graduation Ceremonies Around the World

Sweden

Swedish graduates wear sailor's caps to their graduation ceremony. The ceremony usually starts with singing. Parents arrive and give their children gifts tied with ribbons, and the graduates wear the ribbons around their necks. At the end of the ceremony, there is a parade through the streets of the town, and local people come to congratulate the students.

Japan

In Japan, graduation happens in March, before the new school year. High school students wear their school uniforms for their graduation ceremony. If their school doesn't have a uniform, they wear formal clothes, such as a suit for men and a kimono for women. The principal usually gives a speech. Then the student president gives a speech.

United States

In the US, it's common for a famous person (sometimes a graduate of the university) or a politician to give a speech to congratulate the graduates. In some large American universities, the ceremony happens in a sports stadium. Students normally wear special caps and gowns in the colors of their university or department.

South Africa

Graduates from the University of Witwatersrand in Johannesburg have an interesting musical tradition. The graduation ceremony there starts with a formal procession by the teachers and workers at the university. After that, they play the song "I Got You (I Feel Good)" by James Brown for the students to dance to.

Argentina

Students in Argentina usually wear old clothes for their graduation ceremony. The reason? Family and friends throw sticky or messy food at the graduates, like flour, eggs, ketchup, and soda. It's supposed to bring them good luck!

Unit 3

Track 01

Street Entertainers From Around the World

Juan Eze is a street entertainer from Buenos Aires. "Everywhere I go, people always ask me what my trick is," he says, "but I never tell anyone the secret of my act. Nobody knows." Juan sits for up to four hours at a time without moving, but says he doesn't get bored. What's amazing is that he looks like he's floating. "Everyone thinks I'm doing nothing, but I'm actually watching everything around me."

Marcel Debard, a fire-eater and acrobat, works on the streets of Casablanca. "I started performing about 15 years ago in a circus in Paris. Then someone asked me to help with the fire-eating act and I started to learn how to do it. Is it dangerous? Well, yes, but it's more dangerous for the audience. We have to make sure nobody gets hurt. That's why we blow the fire over the heads of the people."

Huang Jun does a puppet show on the streets of Yangzhou, China. "Puppets are popular forms of entertainment in China, for adults and kids," he explains. "In most puppet shows around the world, no one sees the person controlling the puppets. In Chinese puppet shows, everybody can see everything. It's part of the entertainment—to see how we make the puppets move."

Track 02

Host: As part of our look at careers in the music industry, I'm talking to music producer Scott Fleming. Scott, how did you get into the music industry? Did you use to be in a band?
Scott: Well ... no, I didn't. Actually, I started as a sound technician. I used to check the sound at music concerts. It was hard work!
Host: I bet!
Scott: Also, I used to work as a DJ in a club, and then I went into music production.
Host: And what does a music producer do?
Scott: I help bands produce their songs. We go into the studio together–me, the lead vocalist, the backup singers, the band–and record the song.
Host: And do you write the songs?
Scott: No, that's the job of the songwriter. Bands used to write their own music, but not so much these days.
Host: And what's the most important change in the music industry?
Scott: I think it's probably the importance of music videos. Before MTV started in 1981, people used to listen to music on the radio. Bands used to only record music, but with the start of MTV, they needed to make music videos too.
Host: Why?
Scott: Because the music video was important for marketing. Look at the music video for "Thriller" by Michael Jackson. It was 13 minutes long, and it changed the way people thought about music. I was 14 at the time of "Thriller." It was awesome.
Host: It seems these days people go crazy for the dances in the videos. In 2012, "Gangnam Style," a popular music video from Korea, became world famous.

Scott: Exactly. That's the power of the internet. YouTube started around 2005. Now anybody can make a music video, post it to YouTube, and become successful. People didn't use to do that.

Host: You're right. I read that "Despacito" was the first music video to have over three billion views on YouTube. That happened in August of 2017.

Scott: Yeah, amazing.

Host: Well, thanks for taking the time to talk to us, Scott.

Scott: You're welcome. Thanks for having me.

Track 03

1 A: Did you use to work in marketing?
B: No, I used to work in information technology.

2 A: Did you use to walk to the office?
B: No, I used to take the bus.

3 A: Did your parents use to own a restaurant?
B: No, they used to own a bakery.

Track 04

Speaker 1

I used to watch TV with my mom and dad, but now we all like different shows. They really like police dramas, but I think they're boring! I like streaming shows over the internet. I watch programs from all over the world. Some are in Spanish, but I watch TV shows in English too, and that helps me learn English. I love sitting on my sofa, watching TV.

Speaker 2

I don't watch a lot of TV. I'm very busy at work, so I don't have much time. When I look for things to watch, everything I like is on late at night and I go to bed early. I really like comedy shows, so I watch them on my tablet on demand. I like watching them when I'm eating breakfast. On the weekend, I sometimes binge-watch episodes of a show I like.

Speaker 3

I never watch TV. I think there are too many commercials, and I get bored waiting for them to end. I like watching stuff on YouTube, though. Or I download shows and watch those on my smartphone. I usually watch them on the bus on the way to and from school.

Speaker 4

When I was a kid, I only used to watch TV shows on Saturday mornings. We had a black and white TV. When I was about 12 we got a color one. It was great watching in color! But there used to be only a few channels, and there wasn't that much to watch. As my children grew up, I remember watching a lot of TV shows with them. I still watch TV with my daughter or granddaughter, but we usually watch something on cable.

Track 05

Let's Go to the Movies!

Nowadays, large movie theaters (called multiplexes) are everywhere. They have many screens showing different movies. They show 2D and 3D movies. Some show IMAX movies on giant-sized screens. Some also stream live theater shows or music concerts. In addition, some movie theaters that used to sell only popcorn and candy now have restaurants or cafés where you can enjoy a meal before or after the show. Because of competition from TV movies and home entertainment, movie theaters must find new ways to get people back into their seats.

Some movie theaters now provide an experience where the audience dresses in costumes or sings along to the music. Outdoor or rooftop movie theaters are popular in some cities in the summer. You can also go to a drive-in movie theater (where you watch the movie in your car). There are about 400 drive-in movie theaters in the US today, although they're not as popular as in the 1950s and '60s.

In the past, almost everyone went to the movies. No one had a TV, so it was an exciting form of entertainment. Many beautiful movie theaters opened in the 1920s and '30s when people of all ages went to see the latest Hollywood movie on the big screen. Some of these theaters, such as the Pathé Tuschinski movie theater in Amsterdam and the Orinda Theater in California, are still open today. However, many of the old buildings that used to be movie theaters now have other uses or are closed.

Unit 4

Track 01

What's Your Personality Type?

Are you friendly and outgoing? Or are you the quiet type? Do you like to work as part of a team or do you prefer to work alone? Psychologists try to understand people by studying their personalities. Read on to find out more about four different personality types.

Type As

Type As are often successful, professional people. They are very organized and focused, and they work hard to succeed. Sometimes, they can be impatient with co-workers who aren't as hard-working as they are. They enjoy taking risks, but get stressed easily.

Type Bs

Type Bs are usually easygoing and don't get stressed. They love to spend time with friends and have fun. Usually, they're cheerful and optimistic. Their worst characteristics are that they can be lazy and take a long time to make decisions.

Type Cs

Type Cs are interested in small details and numbers. They are very good problem solvers. They like to be alone and don't always like working as part of a team. They are often shy and find it hard to communicate. Type Cs get as stressed as Type As at work. Take time to relax, Type Cs!

Type Ds

Type Ds aren't as optimistic as Type Bs. In fact, they can be very pessimistic. They often worry, see the negative side of things, and get depressed when things are hard. They like to feel comfortable and don't like to take risks. However, they are patient and hard-working.

Remember that most people are a mix of these different types. It's unusual to find a person who is only one personality type.

Track 02

Jonah isn't as good as Frida at making friends.

I think New Orleans is as interesting as New York.

Track 03

1 I don't think swimming is as difficult as skiing.

2 I'm not as cheerful as my best friend.

3 Learning grammar isn't as easy as learning vocabulary.

Track 04

Lisa: Hello everyone. I think we're ready to begin. Good afternoon and thank you for being here. There are lots of interesting presentations about teamwork this afternoon, so we're very glad you decided to come to this one.

Chris: Yes, thank you. As you can see from the slide, I'm Dr. Chris Baxter and this is my colleague Professor Lisa Perkins. We'd like to talk about working as part of a team …

Lisa: … yes, and the types of personalities you need to make your team the most successful.

Chris: I think that working as part of a team can be one of the most interesting things we do as people.

Lisa: But it's not always easy. People have very different personalities. How do you know who will work well together?

Chris: One answer is to have different types of personalities on the same team. You don't want a team where all the members are workaholics or all the members are risk takers. That is the worst mistake you can make! A good team needs different personalities and skills.

Lisa: At the start of the project, choose the leader. He or she must be the best at solving problems, helping team members communicate, and keeping the main goals in mind. A good leader also knows when to lead and when to ask others to take the lead.

Chris: Most projects also need an expert. An expert has the greatest knowledge about a subject important to the project. The expert will explain all the most important details to the team. For example, many companies have a technology expert to help their employees with new computer technology.

Lisa: Another important member of the team is the creative thinker. The creative thinker is often not the most organized person on the team. But he or she will probably have the best imagination and think of good ideas!

Chris: Remember that these ideas apply to all kinds of areas–at work for sure, but also any area where people come together as a group. That might be a book club, a band, a sports team, or even a classroom.

Track 05

Speaker 1

I think I'm really like my dad. I'm as tall as he is, and we have the same hair and eye color. We're both really bossy. That makes my sister mad! She says I'm always telling her what to do. My sister is like Mom. She looks like her too–they both have brown hair and blue eyes. Also, they are both creative; my sister is studying art and my mom makes her own clothes.

Speaker 2

We're twins, but we're not identical—we don't look like each other at all. He's got brown hair, and I'm blond. He wears glasses, and I don't. I think he looks like our dad, but I look like our mom. Our personalities are similar, though. We're both very adventurous. But I'm not as smart as my brother. He's the smartest person I know.

Speaker 3

People say I look like my aunt. We both have brown eyes and we're both small. Maybe that's why people sometimes think I am her and she is me! She's only six years older than me, so people think we're sisters. She doesn't look like my mom, so it's funny that I look like her. I'm like her in personality, too–we're both a little selfish. I think that's because we both have lots of brothers and sisters!

Speaker 4

When I was born, everyone said I looked like my grandfather! But now that I'm older, they all say I look like my dad. He's bald, and so am I. I guess I'm the tallest in the family, although my dad's tall too. Our personalities are very different. I'm easygoing, but my dad's very strict. Maybe it's because he was a teacher.

Track 06

Lana: Thanks for coming to the meeting. I made notes on the things we need to do. I think we need to focus on this year's fundraiser and organize it.
Ben: A fundraiser? We tried that last year. You know, we spent a lot of money on T-shirts, and we didn't make any money. I think that's a bad idea.
Lana: How much money did we make? And how much did we lose? Alex?
Alex: I have that information right here. We spent $456 on T-shirts, and we made $153. We had a lot of T-shirts that didn't sell. We also spent $120 on food and drink.
Marta: I think fundraisers are fun! I had a great time at the one last year and I think people enjoyed it. OK, so we didn't sell many T-shirts, but maybe we can do something different this year, like have a raffle or a popcorn stand.
Ben: A popcorn stand? I hate popcorn.
Marta: OK, maybe not popcorn. How about we sell cookies? Everyone loves cookies! I can make some.
Alex: Maybe we should find out how much the ingredients cost and how many we need to make. I'm happy to do that.
Lana: Those are all interesting ideas, but I think we need to focus on two things. First, we need to decide on a date for the fundraiser and second, which person can do which job. I think that would be very useful. Alex, take notes, please …

Unit 5

Track 01

Clerk: Bonjour, Hôtel Paris.
Shiro: Hello. Uh … Do you speak English?
Clerk: Of course, sir. Good morning. How can I help you?
Shiro: Good morning. My name is Shiro Ito. My wife and I have a reservation for four nights starting tomorrow, but we have a problem. Your website says that check-in time is two o'clock, but our flight arrives at eight a.m. We'd like to check in at about eleven o'clock if possible.
Clerk: We probably won't have rooms before two, but I'll check to see if any rooms might be ready early. One moment, sir ... I'm sorry, Mr. Ito, but I can't check you in at eleven. However, I can check you in at 1:30, and I can give you a voucher for a free lunch in our restaurant. They have a very nice buffet.
Shiro: That's fine, thank you. We'll eat lunch while we wait.
Clerk: Good. We'll take care of your luggage at the front desk while you have lunch. I think you'll like our restaurant. The food is excellent, and you won't feel so tired if you have some of our good French coffee!
Shiro: I'm sure we'll enjoy the meal, but I won't have coffee because I want to sleep in the afternoon.
Clerk: I understand, sir. Have a good flight, and we'll see you tomorrow.
Shiro: Thanks for your help.
Clerk: You're welcome, Mr. Ito.

Track 02

Conversation 1

Zara: OK, let's plan the party. First, the date.
Lucas: Well, the course ends on June fifth, so how about Saturday, June ninth?
Zara: That sounds good. It's going to be a big party. Where can we have it?
Mika: What about having it in the auditorium here in the institute? I think they'll give us permission to use it.
Zara: That's a good idea, Mika. Could you talk to the director about that?
Mika: Yes. I'll talk to her tomorrow morning.
Zara: Great. Thanks, Mika. What about music, food, and≈drinks?
Lucas: I'll bring the music. I can make playlists, and I'll bring my big speakers.
Zara: Awesome. Now, food and drinks?
Lucas: Can I make a suggestion?
Zara: Of course.
Lucas: Why don't we ask each class to bring their own food and drinks?
Zara: Perfect. Next—invitations! Lucas, you're a designer. Can you design an invitation?
Lucas: Sure, no problem.
Mika: I'll let you know about the auditorium tomorrow.
Lucas: OK. Can you text me?
Mika: Yes, of course.
Zara: OK. That's it for now. Let's meet again next week.

Conversation 2

Ms. Jenkins: Good morning, Zara.
Zara: Good morning, Ms. Jenkins. Could I talk to you for a minute?
Ms. Jenkins: Yes, of course. Come in.
Zara: Thanks. We're planning a party for the end of the course. May we use the auditorium for it?
Ms. Jenkins: When is the party?
Zara: On Saturday, June ninth.
Ms. Jenkins: We have an event in the auditorium the morning of the ninth, but you may use it in the evening.
Zara: Oh, thank you very much, Ms. Jenkins!
Ms. Jenkins: One thing, you can't stay after 10 p.m.
Zara: That's fine, but can four or five of us stay after 10 to clean up the auditorium?
Ms. Jenkins: Yes, you can. I'll let Mr. Carter know.
Zara: Thank you, Ms. Jenkins. I think it will be a great party.
Ms. Jenkins: You're welcome, Zara. Have fun!

Track 03

1 I can make a cake.
2 May I invite my boyfriend?
3 Could you help me, please?
4 I can design an invitation.
5 I won't have coffee.
6 We can't invite friends.

Track 04

Susana: I sent an RSVP to accept Amy's wedding invitation. I'm excited about her wedding!
Jessica: Me too. It's going to be fun!
Susana: Can you tell me about weddings here? I mean, what should I wear?
Jessica: Well, the wedding is in the afternoon, and it's outside, so it isn't very formal, but people usually dress up for weddings.
Susana: OK. I'll wear my new blue dress.
Jessica: Oh, yeah, that dress will be perfect.
Susana: And can you give me some ideas for a wedding gift?
Jessica: Go to the gift registry online and buy one of the gifts on the list. They'll send it to Amy's house.
Susana: Oh, that's easy. Um, am I also invited to the wedding reception?
Jessica: Of course. They're getting married at the Green River Events Center, so the reception is at the same place, right after the wedding ceremony.
Susana: Um, could I go to the wedding with you? I don't have a car.
Jessica: Sure. Rick and I will give you a ride.
Susana: Great. Thanks, Jessica.

Track 05

Social Customs in the US

When you travel to another country, it is important to understand the customs of the country. Here are some useful tips for visitors to the US.

Greetings

- When Americans meet someone for the first time, especially in business situations, they usually shake hands. Young people do not usually shake hands in informal situations. Kissing on the cheek is not a common form of greeting.
- At small social events, Americans sometimes greet each person, but normally people say hello to the group in general.
- Use a person's title (Mr., Ms., Dr.) and last name in business situations or when the other person is much older than you. Never use a title with a first name.

Social Events

- Do not accept an invitation to an event if you don't plan to go. Simply say something like, "I'm sorry, but I have plans that evening. Thanks for the invitation."
- For a dinner party, arrive on time or no more than 5 or 10 minutes late. For an informal party, you can arrive and leave at any time.
- It is typical to take a small gift like flowers or chocolate to a dinner party but not to more informal events.

Food and Restaurants

- In restaurants, Americans often divide the bill so that everyone pays an equal part. If someone says, "My treat," or "I'll get it," that person will pay the bill. Don't argue. Just thank the person.
- If you invite someone to go out to eat, ask if there are foods that they can't eat or don't like before you choose a restaurant.
- Americans often have potluck dinners. This means that everyone brings a large dish to share.

Tipping

- In the US, the normal amount to tip in a restaurant is about 15%, but 20% is common in a very good restaurant. You don't have to tip in fast-food or self-service restaurants. For groups of six people or more, restaurants sometimes add the tip to the bill.
- It is common to tip taxi drivers about 15%.
- In hotels, tip car valets and bellhops $2.00 to $3.00.

Unit 6

Track 01

The Status Quo Bias—Why People Don't Like Change!

If you prefer the status quo, you don't like change. You prefer things to stay the same. Psychologists call this the status quo bias. Many people have a status quo bias, but some people really like change.

Joe and Elena are both 35 years old, but they have very different attitudes about change. Joe has lived in the same city in the same apartment since 2005. He has been with the same company for 12 years. He hasn't bought a new phone for five years, and he has had his car since 2010. Elena has moved three times in the past two years, and she has had four different jobs since 2012. She has worked in her current job for two years, but she thinks she'll probably look for a new job next year.

There are some advantages to the status quo. Life is less stressful in your comfort zone. You feel that you are in control because everything is familiar. There are no risks! However, it can be a good idea to leave your comfort zone and take some risks. This can help you in your professional and personal life. How long have you had the same job? Are there other jobs that pay better or are more interesting? Do you sometimes feel bored with your living situation or your social life? How many times have you eaten at the same restaurant, listened to the same music, gone to the same places on the weekend? If the answer is "a lot," try making a few small changes. Go ahead, order something different the next time you go to that restaurant!

Track 02

1 I've studied English for several years.
2 You've been here since four o'clock.
3 She's lived here since November.
4 It's been very hot outside for two weeks.
5 We've been in class for 45 minutes.
6 They've worked here for a long time.

Track 03

Craig: Good morning, and welcome to *Consider This*. I'm your host, Craig Smith. Today my guests and I are talking about our bucket lists. A bucket list is a list of things that you want to do before a certain age or during your life. For example, I've never flown in a helicopter, and I would like to do that. Jake and Laura, have you ever flown in a helicopter?
Jake: No, I haven't, but I've flown in a small plane. It's pretty cool.
Laura: I have. It's really fun because you have a great view of everything.
Craig: What are some of the things on your bucket lists?
Jake: Well, I've never really thought about a bucket list, but you know, I really like singing, and I'm a pretty good singer. I think I'd like to sing at an open-mic session. And … I've never been to Washington, D.C. It's the capital of my country, so I'd like to do that.
Laura: I really like cars, and I've never driven a sports car. I would love to drive something like a Porsche or a Maserati.
Craig: Wow, that's interesting! OK, after a commercial break, I'm going to talk about how to make a bucket list.

Track 04

I have a couple of tips for making a bucket list. First, try to be realistic. Your list should include things that you think are possible. For example, traveling into space is probably not possible, so traveling to Europe is probably a better option. Next, don't include too many things on your list. You probably won't have time to do all the things on a very long list. One idea is to have one or two big things, like traveling around the world, and several smaller things, like buying a car or moving to another city. Thanks for listening, and good luck with your bucket list!

Track 05

Host: Good afternoon. For today's episode of *Changing Cities*, I'm in Pittsburgh, Pennsylvania. Thanks for inviting me to visit your hometown, Amy. It's beautiful here!
Amy: Yes, it's beautiful now, but it has changed a lot.
Host: Really? How has it changed?
Amy: Pittsburgh was a very industrial city in the past, and it was really polluted. They've really cleaned it up.
Host: Oh, wow. How long has it been this way?
Amy: Since the 1980s, I think. That's when the factories closed and the city started to change.
Host: So what kinds of changes have happened?
Amy: Oh, lots of things. They've created a lot of green spaces with walking trails and playgrounds. They've also put in pedestrian areas and created bike lanes, so now people walk and bike a lot more.
Host: That's really cool. Hey, what are all those people doing around that truck?
Amy: Oh, that's a food truck. Do you have those in your city?
Host: No, we don't.
Amy: Food trucks have become very popular in the US. They have lots of different kinds of food, and it's fast and not very expensive.
Host: That's a great idea!
Amy: That truck has Chinese food. Do you want some?
Host: Yeah, I'm hungry!

Track 06

Guest Opinion: Tourist in Your Own Town

By Lynn Williams

I have decided to become a tourist in my own town and the areas near my town. I read an article that said that many people do not know their own towns, and I thought, "That's me!" I've lived here for 15 years, but I always do the same things and go to the same places. I did some research about activities and places in and near my town, and I've made a list of things that I've never done, or that I haven't done in a long time:

- I've never gone to a high school sports event.
- I've been to the history museum only once, several years ago.
- I've never seen the sunset from Pine Mountain.
- There are about 20 restaurants that I've never tried.
- I've never shopped in the farmer's market.
- I haven't taken a walk on the trail next to the river in five years.

Those are only a few of the things on my list. I imagine that it's the same for almost everyone. We all have our routines, and we never do or see a lot of the fun, interesting things near us. So start a sentence with "I've never …" and see how many ways you can complete it. Do some research to find out what there is to do and see in your area. Then go out and become a tourist in your own town!

Macmillan Education
4 Crinan Street
London N1 9XW
A division of Macmillan Education Limited

Companies and representatives throughout the world

Speak Your Mind Level 2A Student's Book
ISBN 978-1-380-03125-9
Speak Your Mind Level 2A Student's Book + access to Student's App and access to Digital Workbook
ISBN 978-1-380-03123-5
Speak Your Mind Level 2A Student's Book + access to Student's App ISBN 978-1-380-03122-8

Written by Mickey Rogers, Joanne Taylore-Knowles and Steve Taylore-Knowles

First published 2020

Designed by QBS Learning
Illustrated by Daniel Deamo (Lemonade) pp. 8, 48; Martina Farrow p. 21; Keith Favazza (Wendy Lynn & Co.); QBS Learning p. 60.
Cover design by therestless.co.uk
Cover photographs by Getty Images/Chatuporn Sornlampoo/EyeEm (background); Shutterstock/leungchopan (lower body), Shutterstock/Dima Sidelnikov (upper body), Shutterstock/ventdusud (window).
Picture research by Fernanda Rocha/Ikonia LLC

Authors' acknowledgements
Mickey, Jo, and Steve would like to thank everyone at Macmillan Education and RedNova Learning who have made this project possible and who have gone the extra mile (literally!) to meet up, work together, and throw around a million ideas, some of which even made their way into the books! Jo and Steve would also like to thank Scout for her patience and understanding and for letting her parents get on with it when they needed to!

The publishers would like to thank all the teachers that piloted and reviewed the series, and a special thanks to Annette Flavel for content and cultural reviews.

The authors and publishers would like to thank the following for permission to reproduce their photographs:
Alamy Stock Photo/Amy Cicconi p. 62(bl), Alamy Stock Photo/a-ts p. 22(7), Alamy Stock Photo/Antony McAulay p. 24(tl), Alamy Stock Photo/parkerphotography p. 28(tr), Alamy Stock Photo/Naho Yoshizawa/Aflo Co., Ltd p. 24(tc); E+/filadendron, TODOR TSVETKOV p. 12(br); **Getty Images**/Aliraza Khatri's Photography p. 34(tl), Getty Images/Markus Altmann p. 14(t), Getty Images/Danilo Andjus p. 12(2), Getty Images/andresr pp. 26(br), 128, Getty Images/eli_asenova p. 12(6), Getty Images/Avalon_Studio p. 22(br), Getty Images/KatarzynaBialasiewicz p. 130, Getty Images/Big Cheese Photo p. 12(1), Getty Images/BJI/Blue Jean Images p. 38(tl), Getty Images/Caiaimage/Martin Barraud p. 38(tml), Getty Images/dlerick p. 22(4), Getty Images/Ola Dusegard p. 62(3), Getty Images/Geber86 p. 32(b), Getty Images/Hero Images pp. 38(tr), 38(a, c), Getty Images/ivotheeditors p. 34(cl), Getty Images/Jamesmcq24 p. 22(5), Getty Images/Juanmonino p. 14(c), Getty Images/Maya Karkalicheva p. 64(t), Getty Images/Eva-Katalin p. 32(c), Getty Images/Ronnie Kaufman p. 40(b), Getty Images/Dennis McColeman p. 64(br), Getty Images/Mike Kemp p. 32(a), Getty Images/kuarmungadd p. 14(b), Getty Images/Artur Lebedev/Contributor p. 61, Getty Images/Loop Images/Craig Joiner p. 62(4), Getty Images/LWA p. 12(3), Getty Images/Emilija Manevska p. 12(8), Getty Images/Maskot p. 62(6), Getty Images/Meridian Studios p. 42(a), Getty Images/Mikeh57 p. 19, Getty Images/Milkos p. 38(tmr), Getty Images/Josef Mohyla p. 18(tr), Getty Images/Tara Moore p. 44, Getty Images/ollo p. 34(tr), Getty Images/Alex Segre/Contributor p. 64(cr), Getty Images/Ariel Skelley p. 24(tr), Getty Images/Smith Collection/Gado/Contributor p. 34(cr), Getty Images/Tinpixels p. 48(cr), Getty Images/Omar Vega/Contributor p. 8, Getty Images/Westend61 p. 48(tr), Getty Images/Todd Wright p. 42(b); **Shutterstock**/aerogondo2 p. 12(4), Shutterstock/amasterphotographer p. 58, Shutterstock/Claudia K p. 42(c), Shutterstock/design56 p. 22(1)Shutterstock/Dmitry Bruskov p. 62(7), Shutterstock/Vasiliy Budarin p. 27, Shutterstock/DNF Style p. 12(7), Shutterstock/Orest Drozda p. 52, Shutterstock/Kaspars Grinvalds p. 12(5), Shutterstock/ImageFlow p. 66, 132, Shutterstock/Images By Kenny p. 22(6), Shutterstock/Teerasak Ladnongkhun p. 22(2), Shutterstock/lassedesignen p. 5, Shutterstock/Lucky Team Studio p. 132, Shutterstock/Mariyana M p. 22(8), Shutterstock/MinDof p. 18(tl), Shutterstock/Luciano Mortula - LGM p. 62(2), Shutterstock/pathdoc p. 37, Shutterstock/Pavel L Photo and Video p. 30, Shuttestock/Sean Pavone p. 62(br), Shutterstock/Valeri Potapova p. 62(1), Shutterstock/pryzmat p. 62(8), Shutterstock/Rawpixel.com pp. 54, 75, Shutterstock/rozbyshaka p. 17, Shutterstock/SAPhotog p. 28(cl), Shuttestock/S.Borisov p. 62(5), Shutterstock/Panwasin seemala p. 28(cr), Shutterstock/pathdoc p. 15, Shutterstock/Romolo Tavani p. 57, Shutterstock/Binh Thanh Bui p. 22(3), Shutterstock/viputae p. 47, Shutterstock/WAYHOME studio pp. 32(d), 42(d).

Additional Sources:
p. 36, "What's the average survey response rate? [2018 benchmark]," by Nigel Lindemann, October 24, 2018, Survey Anyplace blog. p. 66, "How to Become an Architect: Education and Career Roadmap," Study.com website.

Printed and bound in Mexico
by Compañía Editorial Ultra, S.A. de C.V.

2021 2020
12 11 10 09